Mor

CURIOSITIES

Bolsover Castle (no. 169)

# of DERBYSHIRE
and the PEAK DISTRICT

by
Frank Rodgers
with photography by the author

Published by Derbyshire Countryside Ltd., Heritage House, Lodge Lane, Derby, DE1 3HE

Front cover: The Watch House at Bradfield (*no. 138*), Statue on pillar of Golden Gates at Elvaston (*no. 87*), Cider Mill at Sapperton Manor (*no. 96*), Monks' Bridge, near Egginton (*no. 93*).

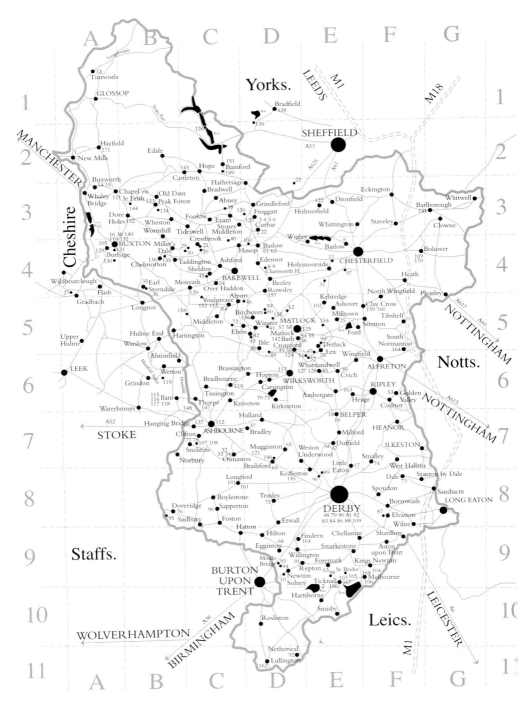

Based upon the Ordnance Survey mapping with the permission of
The Controller of Her Majesty's Stationery Office   © Crown copyright 399531

2

Contents

3

The introduction opposite gives some idea of the scope of this book and how this second book came about. The use of the contents page together with the map references will help to find the features shown in the following pages. Thus by browsing through this collection of miscellaneous and fascinating subjects in advance one can plan visits to find them.

Introduction

When *Curiosities of the Peak District and Derbyshire* was first published in 1979 it was an immediate success, going to three reprints. In 1995 a revised and slightly enlarged fourth edition was published by Derbyshire Countryside Ltd. under the new title *Curiosities of Derbyshire and the Peak District*. This is now out of print but its success has prompted me to compile this second volume entitled *More Curiosities of Derbyshire and the Peak District* which follows the same theme, 'including features natural and otherwise which arouse curiosity'. Again the information in the captions has been gleaned from the many contacts made and also from my very large collection of books too numerous to mention here. In many cases old photographs have been retained giving an added historical interest and, where necessary, the subjects revisited.

I thank my wife for her help and companionship during our rambles with a camera during the past sixty years and also

Entrance to Repton School

our two sons. They later helped in the compilation of the map. We thank all those friendly people who allowed us to take photographs and never seemed wearied with our questioning! I hope readers will find as much pleasure as we did if they follow in our footsteps around our beautiful countryside.

Frank Rodgers

On Froggatt Edge

5

own *mind never to touch intoxicating drink
again.'* In 1984 the derelict cottage was renovated and the crumbling tablet renewed.

2 Village Lock Up   E9

The village lock-up in Ticknall is almost hidden by bushes and easily missed. The inmates of these small prisons were usually drunks, put there for their own safety or because they were a nuisance. Sometimes they came out more drunk than when they went in, for a common prank was to supply them with drink through a straw by way of the small window. More serious offenders were held while waiting for transport to local assizes. Probably the most famous inmate of these tiny prisons was Shakespeare, put there for poaching – many examples of these lock-ups still stand in our villages.

1 The Drunkard's Reform Cottage   A2

The tablet seen to the right of the bedroom window of this cottage in Dyehouse Lane in New Mills reads as follows:

A DRUNKARD'S REFORM

A working man a teetotaller for ten years who was formerly a notorious drinker and notorious poacher, has recently invested his sober earnings in the purchase of the town prison which he has converted into a comfortable dwelling house. Frequently an inmate of the prison whilst a drunkard and a poacher, he is now owner of the whole and occupier of the premises.

Thomas Handford
AD 1854

What made Thomas become teetotal is recorded in a magazine article published in 1899. It seems that he was in the *Cock Inn* which stood next to the prison when his drinking companion suddenly collapsed and died. *'This awful visitation upset Handford to such an extent that he walked out of the house and resolved in his*

3 A Walt Disney House   D3

This quaint Disney-type house standing on the hillside above Curbar village in the Derwent Valley always arouses curiosity. Its conical roof is set cleverly on a square building and there is a chimney and two floors. There has been much speculation about its origin and it has been described as a lock-up. It was often thought to be a halfway house for prisoners crossing the moors from the prisons at Sheffield and Stafford. However when the author met the late Clarence Daniel of Eyam some years ago this well-known local historian told him that it was built as a bath house for the Methodist Cliff College nearby. When the bath house was abandoned it was inhabited by an old sailor who spent his time making those model ships which are inserted into bottles. Mr Daniel remembers a model ship fixed to a spike on the top of the building. Today this delightful little house graces the garden of a new house built close by and is inaccessible but clearly seen from a public footpath which passes nearby. This path climbs the hillside and passes the Plague Graves shown in the following entry.

4 Plague Graves at Curbar   D3

A sad note is struck beside these lonely graves in the open fields below Curbar Edge, for they are the resting place of the Cundy family of Grislowfields Farm nearby. The name of the farmer Thomas Cundy is indicated on one stone by the initials TC and the date 1632, and in a similar way that of his wife and their three children. In that year the bubonic plague came to Curbar and the Cundys were the only victims, unlike the devastation which came to Eyam just 33 years later.

5 Mystery Device at Curbar D3

Built into a wall beside the road in Curbar village there is a curious feature, and it is suggested that it originally stood in a farmyard. Readers may have their own ideas of its purpose, but having been brought up on a farm and spent much time holding sacks open while they were filled, the author suggests the following. A sack would be hung down through the hole in the projecting stone, its top edge being held by a metal ring. This would be clamped down by a rod passed through the two metal rings. The author has not seen a similar device elsewhere, and wonders if it was the brainchild of one farmer?

6 Two Restored Pinfolds D3/E4

Most villages had their pinfolds or pounds where stray animals were impounded by the pounder until claimed, on payment of a fee, by the owner. Many of these still stand, generally in various stages of neglect or forgotten. Not so these two fine restored examples the first of which may be seen beside the road a short distance up the hill from Calver Mill seen in the next illustration. Circular with high walls of limestone it once clearly proclaimed *The Pinfold* on the gate. The second stands just outside the village of Barlow north of Chesterfield and is completely different,

being square and made of gritstone. The name *Pinfold* is carved on the lintel over the doorway, but the word Barlow has been crudely chipped away. This removal of the name of the village came about in the early days of the Second World War when invasion was threatened and local authorities were told to remove any evidence useful to airborne invaders. A colourful little plaque informs us that the pinfold is in the care of the Chesterfield Civic Society.

7 'Colditz' Mill   D3

'Why do I feel that I've been here before when I know that I haven't ?' This scrap of conversation, overheard on the old bridge over the River Derwent in Calver, reminded the author that the gaunt cotton mill among the trees nearby was the setting for the film 'Colditz' seen by millions of viewers on the television. Built in 1803 it replaced an earlier cotton mill of 1785 burnt down in 1802. A corn mill originally stood on the site. Cotton production ceased in the 1920s, and the area round the mill has been attractively landscaped. Through the years the mill had several different owners, and one of these, probably Horatio Mason, built the school at Stocking Farm nearby. If so, he should join Strutt and Arkwright and others who had the welfare of their employees at heart. The school has a bell turret and outside steps supported on

pillars and is passed by a footpath which crosses the fields from the mill to New Bridge higher up the valley. Here is a weir built to divert the waters of the river into the long goit down to the mill. Yet another query, had Stocking Farm anything to do with the mill, did the word 'stocking' come from livestock?

8 Bridges' Secrets   D4

Two miles below Curbar Bridge the River Derwent enters Chatsworth Park where it is crossed by two of the loveliest bridges in the county. Each has its own unusual feature, perhaps passed unnoticed. The elegant structure of three arches and adorned by statues was designed by the architect James Paine and is seen here close by Chatsworth House. When the author took this photograph about 50 years ago he was attracted by the activity of swallows beneath the bridge, and was amazed on finding their nests anchored to the stalactites hanging there. The water dripping from the arch is obviously impregnated with lime (no.55). A recent visit showed it is very difficult to see beneath the bridge due to the growth of trees in the intervening years, but it is quite possible that the birds still use this very unusual building site.

9 An Unusual Deer Fence D4

Where the Derwent leaves Chatsworth Park it passes beneath another of Paine's bridges. Beeley Bridge was built in 1760, two years before the one shown above and totally different in style. A graceful single arch is too narrow for anything wider than a single carriage, and an attractive lodge close by seems to indicate that it was originally a private road into the park. It is also steeply 'humpbacked' so that one cannot see approaching traffic and traffic lights, (the first in the county?) are needed on this now busy road through the park. A stile beside the bridge gives access to a footpath which crosses the fields to Beeley Village and in the field one can see hanging from the arch a fence of hanging chains which prevent deer escaping from the park.

10 Hoskin's Folly D9

Bladon Castle stands high on a ridge to the west of Newton Solney near Burton-on-Trent, and was originally called Hoskin's Folly when it was built shortly after 1800. Built of brick, it was designed by Sir Jeffry Wyatville for Abraham Hoskin whose family owned a small brickyard behind the Brickmakers Arms in the village. Following complaints that this sham served no purpose a house was built behind its impressive façade which still arouses interest and curiosity in travellers who climb the hill out of Newton Solney on their way to Burton-on-Trent (shown as Bladon Castle on the Landranger Ordnance Map).

11 Gladwin's Folly E4

Belmont House is a curious mixture of architectural styles, giving it the name locally of Gladwin's Folly. It stands in Holymoorside near Chesterfield near the junction of Holymoor Road with the Baslow Road and was built by General Henry Gladwin in the 18th century. It is said that he built the curious tower so that he could fire a canon at Gladwin's Mark, a farm standing on a hill across the valley. The strange flying buttresses built against the tower are in fact chimneys built there to counter down-draught. There is a ballroom and the rooms have secret panelling which would have been exciting when it became a children's home run by the County Council in 1953 (shown as Belmont on the Landranger Ordnance Map).

12 Sydnope Stand   D5

Standing high and isolated among the wooded hills to the east of Darley Dale, this unusual house arouses curiosity in all who pass by. It was built in 1865 by the owners of Sydnope Hall as a folly or eyecatcher replacing a hunting lodge there. With its church-like tower, castellated walls and Gothic windows it certainly creates a very unusual home (shown on the Landranger Ordnance Map).

13 Monkey House   A1

This tall house beside the Longdondale road just outside Tintwistle in the far north of the county cannot be recognised as a toll house yet that was its origin. When refusal to extend it in the usual way was made, it was decided to heighten it, and for some reason is called Monkey House.

14 Dolly Pit Engine House A3

An unusual and very attractive house in Buxworth near Whaley Bridge was originally the engine house of the Dolly Pit Colliery.

15 Unusual Steps   A3

The Peak Forest Canal extended to Buxworth where there are extensive remains of basins and wharves indicating a very busy port. These unusual steps gave access to and from the canal and roadway. They are formed by 'through' stones and had to be negotiated carefully, and seem to be indicative of the rough nature of the workers here. Among other activities, the stone from the Buxton Lime Quarries brought down on the Peak Forest Tramway was transferred here to the boats.

16 Peak Forest Tramway   A3

This wagon wheel and portion of flanged rail can be seen in the museum at Buxton. They came from the tramway which ran from Buxton down Barmoor Clough to the Peak Forest Canal at Buxworth mentioned in the previous entry. The rails, three feet long, were made by the Benjamin Outram Company and were attached to the stone sleepers by a large nail driven into a wooden plug in the stone block. A similar plateway was used from the canal at Little Eaton to the coal mines at Denby (no.17).

Photo: courtesy of Buxton Tram Museum

17 Little Eaton Clock House E7

This unimposing and conventional type house is hidden behind modern business premises in Little Eaton and is easily missed. It is situated opposite the New Inn public house in Duffield Road, and the Clock House, as it is called, is the only evidence of an important and once busy wharf here. It was the terminus of the northern branch of the Derby Canal which made a connection here with the 'plateway' or 'gangroad', an early railway which carried coal from the pits at Denby and Kilburn. The wagons ran on short flanged rails similar to those used in Barmoor Clough (no. 16) and ran straight onto the rails from the road. This seems to indicate that this is how the present standard railway gauge of 4' 8½" came about, for when the flange was transferred from the rail to the wheel this gauge had already been established. The wagons were horse-drawn, and here at Little Eaton, where these two early forms of transport met, there were workshops, stables, offices and a weighbridge necessary for the transfer. The Clock House was built in 1793, and no doubt the clock was important. The gangroad ended in 1908 and anyone so interested may find evidence of it in the form of small stone sleepers built into walls along its route up the valley of the Bottle Brook. Of the canal only dried up portions of it remain, but the towpath is now a pleasant cycle track into Derby, a route which it is intended will continue along the derelict canal to Swarkestone. Here it links with a disused railway to Melbourne.

18 Belper Nailers   E7

Mention 'The Nailers' in Belper and most people think of the town's football club, but strangers may not know that it had taken its name from the major industry of making nails centuries ago. It dates back to at least the 14th century, long before the Strutts left their mark with the huge mills beside the Derwent (next entry). It was originally a cottage industry like the stockingers' houses still standing at Derby, Crich and Ashford-in-the-Water but the nail-makers could not work in the houses. A forge was needed and small smithies were built at the bottom of the garden as seen here in Joseph Street. Iron rod was bought from larger smiths and beaten into the various types of nails from the small common types to the larger horseshoe nails and the heavy kind used to hold Outram's flanged plates on his tramways (no. 16). With the introduction of machine-made nails this cottage industry had virtually ceased by 1900 and it is good to see this example preserved.

15

19 No Trouble at T'Mill   E7

The complex of Strutt's mills around the bridge over the Derwent at Belper cannot be missed by the traveller along the A6 road. Around 1800 a covered gangway was built over the Ashbourne Road to connect buildings each side and it was thought prudent to provide gunports covering the road beneath as a defence against possible Luddites. There are three of these, a central one on the Ashbourne side and two on the Belper side, one of which can be seen here high above the small arch, (note the small drinking point beside the arch). Fortunately the machine wreckers never visited these mills. Today the massive East Mill houses the Derwent Visitor Centre where several themes have been developed including the history of framework knitting, cotton spinning and the Belper Nailers. The River Gardens close by are well worth a visit.

20 At Cressbrook Mill   C4

Walkers along the footpath which runs beside the River Wye in Water-cum-Jolly may be puzzled by this church-like building at Cressbrook Mill. The footpath passes between the mill building and Apprentice Row, a line of cottages where orphans who worked in the mill were housed. This building stands at the end of the row of cottages and is thought to have been the chapel where they were given religious teaching. In the terrible days of child slavery when very young children worked long hours and often died before reaching their teens, those at Cressbrook were treated decently. About one mile upstream, at the other end of Water-cum-Jolly, the path passes through the yard of Litton Mill which had a dreadful record of child slavery and cruelty. Apprentice Row later became Pancake Row and is now a row of cottages called Dale View. This photograph shows how the chapel looked many years ago and it has now been restored by the Peak Park Authority.

21 A Seat at Cressbrook C4

Toiling up the steep road which climbs
from Cressbrook Mill to the village of
Cressbrook you will see with surprise and
relief this seat beside the road. Beautifully
designed and fashioned in limestone, it
was erected over 100 years ago to
commemorate Mr Charles Edward Solly,
manager of the mill, who died at the early
age of 33. Through the years it had
become neglected, and when Cressbrook
became a Conservation Area in 1986 the
seat was renovated by the Peak Park
Authority. We have Major J N Solly,
nephew and godson of Charles Solly and
Mr Ben Dawson of Litton Parish Council
to thank for this respite and for the
convenient rest it provides.

22 Gritstone Relics D3

The gritstone edges and moors of
Froggatt, Curbar and Baslow which tower
over the upper Derwent Valley have been
worked for this durable stone through the
centuries. Millstone grit has taken its
name from this stone, and many examples
of millstones, troughs and gateposts still lie
around the moors. To its credit Curbar
village has preserved examples of these in
the village centre with a spring used for
domestic purposes protected from animal
use by slabs placed upright.

23 An Abandoned Trough D3

This trough on Hathersage Moor has
been abandoned as it developed a crack
before it was finished. One can only
imagine the frustration at such a
happening, or marvel at the transporting
of these heavy finished articles from these
lonely moors to some distant farm or to a
foundry in nearby Sheffield.

24 A Circle of Troughs C4

Every farmyard had its water trough and this one high above the River Lathkill at Over Haddon has a circle made up of four segments. Originally it had a pump in the centre, water being pumped from the Lathkill far below. The farm has been converted into a craft centre and the troughs are now an object of curiosity to the many visitors.

25 Trough at the Inn E5

Like the circle of troughs at Over Haddon, this one standing ouside the *Miners Standard* at Milltown near Ashover is probably unique too. Fittingly it also incorporates a mounting block, a combination the author has not found elsewhere in the county.

26 The Twelve Apostles D5

This row of troughs known locally as the Twelve Apostles stand in the little hamlet of Ible high above the Via Gellia. The cottage seen on the right was once a Methodist Chapel, and one wonders if the name of the troughs has any connection. The hamlet, a few farms and cottages, lies astride a single road which climbs steeply from Grange Mill and loops round to wind equally steeply back down into the Via Gellia. The troughs serve the farms and one also thinks of packhorses but there seems no record of a packhorse route hereabouts. Ible lies just within the Peak National Park, for the road through the Via Gellia forms its boundary.

27 On the Packhorse Routes A4

It comes as a surprise to find a row of troughs in lonely places until one realises there is a packhorse route nearby. Those seen here will be found in the Dane Valley on the Derbyshire border with Cheshire on the lonely route which connects the mills in Gradbach below with those in Wildboarclough. These tracks make fine walking routes, often strenuous and these troughs come as a welcome respite as no doubt they did to the packhorses and their drivers long ago.

28 An Iron Trough E6

One cannot travel far in Derbyshire without noticing the stone troughs in the farmyards and villages as shown in the previous pages. This trough in the yard of Holme Farm at Lea near Cromford however, breaks the sequence for it is made of iron. Perhaps unique in the county it is now made attractive with plants which hide an interesting feature inside the trough. A separate casting in the form of a hollow column is bolted in the centre with its top edge at a lower level than the rim of the trough, thus acting as an overflow through the bottom of the trough. A spring higher up the valley supplies the water through a pipeline. The author is indebted to Mr Hugh Sheldon of Lea Hall, who once owned the farm, for this information and who also suggested that the trough was probably made at the Butterley Ironworks, with which the author entirely agreed. One wonders if it is unique, for would they have made only one casting after making the pattern or strickle needed; unless it was made to a special order. One also wonders about the transport of such an awkward and heavy

casting which is one and a half inches thick. Did it come by road from the works at Ripley or along the tortuous route through Butterley Tunnel as described in no. 53 ? Holme Farm is no longer in use as a farm for it has a shop and a prestigious restaurant called *The Coach House*.

29 Hilltop Chimney C4

The narrow gorge of Millers Dale is
almost blocked by Litton Mill mentioned
in no. 20. On the hillside above stands
this circular limestone tower, and should
one climb the footpath which runs nearby
it is revealed as a chimney. This is proved
by an underground flue, now in ruins,
which may be traced down to the mill.
One may assume that a chimney situated
beside the mill deep in the valley would
not 'draw', and now this isolated chimney
seen from afar with the mills out of sight
arouses curiosity.

30 A Detached Cottage Chimney C4

This little cottage standing near the
entrance to Litton Mill mentioned in the
previous entry also has a detached
chimney, and one wonders why. Close by
is a shelter with round pillars, perhaps
built for workers at the mill who arrived
on horseback.

32 A very Ornate Chimney C7

31 Oldest Industrial Chimney   E4

Standing on the hills above the Amber Valley and not far from the restored windmill seen in no. 163 this chimney is much more sinister than that at Litton seen in no. 29. It is all that is left of large lead smelting works which stood here, and is said to be the oldest industrial chimney in England. It was built on this isolated spot because the fumes, called the belland, given off are poisonous and poisoned the ground itself. It was built about the mid-1800s by the London Lead Company and smelting continued for almost a century, but today nothing remains but this chimney and a pool which was used to power bellows in an area of disrupted ground. It is shown on the Landranger Ordnance map near the junction of the A 5057 Darley Dale road with the A 532 Chesterfield Road on Stone Edge.

Osmaston Manor was built in Osmaston village just south of Ashbourne in 1819 and demolished in 1966. Nothing remains except the garden terraces and the kitchen gardens which have a most interesting feature. These gardens are now a very successful nursery and here visitors' curiosity is aroused by the ornate 150 feet high Italian-type tower. This is a chimney totally different from those at Litton Mill and Stanedge shown in previous pages. The comment that 'Surely greenhouses don't need one that big' was heard and the speaker assured that it was a communal chimney which had served the whole manor. The house had 70 rooms and a bakehouse, wash-house and a brew-house and a central tunnel carried smoke to the chimney in the garden. The house, and chimney, were designed by H. I. Stevens, the Derby architect, who also designed the church at the other end of the village. Three years after the house was completed the chimney was struck by lightning, but as seen here, still survives to grace the gardens to the delight and curiosity of visitors.

33 Osmaston Thatch C7

Derbyshire has few thatched cottages but Osmaston near Ashbourne has some fine examples; even the Village Hall is thatched. This one stands beside the Pool and the thatcher is proud of his work for it is signed with an 'M', the initial of George Mellor of Cromford. For many years the family have been thatching here in Derbyshire and further afield, and this splendid example is typical of their work.

34 A Horseshoe Seat C7

Yet another example of an old country craft is seen beside the Pool in the shape of a seat made of horseshoes where one can sit and enjoy this tranquil scene in Osmaston.

35 The Quiet Woman B4

The history of inn names is a fascinating one. *The Red Lion* and *The Queen's Head* inns abound but there are others which raise a query or cause a smile, and *The Quiet Woman* must come under the latter. This ancient inn is at Earl Sterndale in the upper Dove Valley near Buxton, and the tale is told of how the publican, of the name Charteris, was so fed up with his wife's chattering that he cut off her head. The sign shows a woman with her head tucked beneath her arm and the words *'Soft Words Turneth Away Wrath'*. The church has the dubious distinction of being the only one in the county which was bombed in the Second World War. One night in 1941 a German bomber, thought to be returning from a raid on Manchester, jettisoned its incendiary bombs over the village, and by an amazing stroke of ill luck hit the church. The roof was burnt out but a wedding booked went ahead with the roof open to the sky. The church which stands opposite *The Quiet Woman*, was restored ten years later.

23

36 A Hilltop Memorial B4

This evenly-shaped hill called High Wheeldon is situated near the village of Earl Sterndale in the upper Dove Valley. Although looking strangely artificial seen from this viewpoint, it is nevertheless quite natural, a cave near the summit proving of great interest to archaeologists. Fragments of pottery from Neolithic times found here show that it was inhabited about 5,000 years ago. The hill is now owned by the National Trust, presented by that great lover of Dovedale and the Manifold Valley, Mr. F. A. Holmes M. A. and J. P. of Buxton, shortly before his death in 1947. He gave it as a memorial to the men and women of the Staffordshire and Derbyshire Regiments who lost their lives in the Second World War, and the author was honoured when Mr Holmes asked him to record it for him in photographs. The author and his wife are seen in this photograph taken about 60 years ago. It is shown on the Landranger Ordnance Map.

37 Hole in the Wall   D7

The strange name *Hole in the Wall* is shown on the Landranger Ordnance Map and the curious will find this scene when visiting the spot at Moor End near Bradley a few miles east of Ashbourne. The reason for building these two cottages spanning the road is open to speculation. It has been suggested that it was a toll house, for the walls facing each other beneath the arch have a blocked-up doorway and small window. Obviously these were used to check passage through the arch, and the fact that there was once a gate here - the hinges remain - seems to confirm this. However there are no windows through which to observe the approaching traffic as in the conventional type of toll house (no. 81). The London to Manchester turnpike road passes through Ashbourne and Bradley is mentioned on its route. However, could it be that the *Hole in the Wall* was a gatehouse to Bradley Hall. The Hall has been converted from extensive stables, originally the home of the Meynell Hunt and there would be extensive traffic through the archway. Not far away is Yeldersley Hall and Yeldersley Old Hall and the author visited his grandparents over 70 years ago who lived in a thatched cottage opposite the Old Hall and remembers the archway looking very much as it does in this photograph taken about fifty years ago. Today it forms a very attractive group with trees and shrubs and is still an object of curiosity.

38 Bretton Race Course   C3

Bretton is a tiny hamlet of a few cottages and an inn situated beside a long fairly straight road high on Eyam Edge north of the village of Eyam.

Long ago the road was known as Bretton Race Course where it was said disputes over horses were settled. These often arose regarding speed, staying power etc. It was also said that horses were trained here for the Sheffield Handicap; no doubt the cleaner air 1,300 feet above sea level here was preferable to that in Sheffield at that time.   No doubt too many wagers were made by the hardy men of the Peak on this hilltop who would then spend the evening in the *Barrel* as it was simply called.   Seen from afar the inn has been a landmark since 1637 and is still very popular, its hanging sign being very unusual as too is the barrel fixed to the front of the building.   There is no place for horse racing among the modern cars on the road today.

39 Lead Mine Coe   E6

Evidence of the ancient industry of lead
mining may be seen all over the Peak
District. Names like coes, rakes, soughs
and stowes all arouse curiosity and readers
may like to see photographs and
explanations of these (nos. 40 & 49). This
is a good example of a coe photographed
years ago near Crich; a simple hut where a
miner kept his tools and clothing.
Sometimes it was built over the mine shaft
with a trapdoor. In this example the shaft
has been covered with a cairn of stones
for safety but when in use would have a
stowe or windlass over it, and in the harsh
laws of those days anyone caught stealing
lead may have his hand nailed to the
stowe. Prospecting for lead could be
carried out anywhere except in a burial
ground or a garden and these small mines
were often owned by a family or even a
single individual. Today many of these
small shafts have been capped with
concrete, but one should always be
cautious and never venture into a grassy
depression where there may be a shaft
covered with now rotten timbers.

40 Lead Rake   C4

Disrupted ground running across the hills
indicates where a lead vein or rake has
been worked by the lead miner. These
rakes have given the name to several place
names like Long Rake and Dirty Rake
and today many are being reworked for
the residue fluorspar. Again there may be
an occasional mineshaft hidden in the
depressions – they are not playgrounds.
The photograph shows Tideswell Rake on
Longstone Edge north of Hassop.

41 Original Mill Close Mine
D5

The scars left by the famous Mill Close Mine can hardly be missed and arouse curiosity in strangers passing through Darley Dale. Until its closure in 1939 it had been the most productive and richest lead mine in the world. However there was a predecessor, for in the mid 1800s the Old Mill Close Mine, or Watts Shaft, had been sunk in Clough Wood north of Wensley. Not entirely successful, it did however lead to the discovery of a rich seam to the north, and the famous Mill Close Mine was sunk there in Darley Dale. Little evidence remains of the original Watts Shaft except the great mass of masonry seen here where in the late 1880s a photograph shows great activity. This building housed a steam engine, the beam moving up and down in the large opening and operating a pump in the mine shaft situated in front. This was eight feet in diameter and also gave access to the mine. Today these remains may arouse curiosity only in the ramblers, perhaps unaware of their archaeological importance.

42 The Miners Standard   D5

The valley in which the Watts Shaft shown in the previous photograph is situated runs up to Winster, once an important lead mining centre. The area is littered with old lead mines, and it is not surprising that here stands the *Miners Standard Inn* which takes its name from the standard measuring dish held in the Moot Hall at Wirksworth. A tablet over the inn door shows that it was built in 1633 together with the initials EP, EP and FP, and should you be curious about these you may be told that they stand for '*Every Person Entering Pays For a Pint*'. In fact they are the initials of the original owners of the inn, Edith, Ella and Frank Prince who built it. It is shown on the Landranger Ordnance Map as the PH beside the B5056 where a secondary road branches off to drop into Winster.

43 A Lead Ore House   D5

This simple building also stands beside the
B5056 just above the *Miners Standard*
shown in the previous entry and is usually
passed unnoticed by the motorist. Here
the smaller mine owners 'banked' their
lead while awaiting its collection; it was
tipped down a chute from outside which
was approached up a grassy mound. Large
doors at the front have been replaced by a
grill so that one can see the chute and
vaulted interior, and here a notice informs
us that it is the finest example in
Derbyshire and was in use as recently as
50 years ago. Unfortunately the notice
carries no date. A small settlement called
Islington Green, thought to be miners,
once stood astride Islington Lane behind
the *Miners Standard*. Now a field lane this
was an important route in Anglo-Saxon
times for it is a portion of The Portway
which crossed the county from the south
east to the north west.

44 A Lead Drift Mine   D5

The lead mine shafts and rakes shown in
nos. 39 and 40 are dangerous places and so
too are the drift mines such as the one
shown here in the Via Gellia. Often these
lead to vertical shafts cut to a lower level
and one should not venture inside. This
photograph was taken many years ago and
the shaft may have been secured as have
many of the shafts on the hills above.
Several Roman lead 'pigs' from the 2nd
century AD have been unearthed in this
area, and where the road called Clatterway
runs down from Bonsall to the road in the
Via Gellia there is the popular public house
The Pig of Lead.

45 Magpie Mine C4

Whilst evidence of the lead mining activities is scattered all over the Peak District, the stark ruins of the Magpie Mine which stand on the hills above the village of Sheldon near Bakewell are the most impressive. Here a number of veins merged and a cluster of shafts sunk under different ownership. Disputes were inevitable when miners broke through into neighbouring workings. A tragedy occurred when they tried to smoke each other out and a curse was put on the mine, taken seriously in those days. The main shaft is over 700 feet deep, and with the usual problem of flooding a sough was cut to the River Wye over a mile away. The outlet can be seen in Great Shacklow Wood where it is crossed by a footpath. Magpie Mine has a long history thought to date back 300 years and there is much to see here. A number of footpaths converge on the area which is the Field Centre for the Peak District Mines Historical Society and one is grateful for permission to look around, but do take great care and keep to the paths. It is shown on the Landranger Ordnance Map.

46 Smelting at Alport D5

Not all smelting was carried out in isolated places to minimise lead poisoning (no. 31) and two of the largest smelting works were at Lea Bridge near Cromford (no. 47) and Alport seen here. Below the village and on the hillside above the River Bradford are the remains of flues and ruined buildings so overgrown they are seen only in the wintertime when the undergrowth has died down. They were built about 1840 and ran for less than 50 years. The ground is private and the ruins can be seen only from the road which runs along the other side of the valley.

29

47 Smelting at Lea Bridge E5

These smelting works stood beside the road which drops from Lea village to Lea Bridge. This was one of the largest smelting works in Derbyshire, and by the end of the 18th century all the lead from the Derbyshire mines was smelted here. It was developed by the Nightingale family of Florence Nightingale fame, and was later taken over by Joseph Wass but work ceased about 1938 and within ten years all the buildings had been demolished and only this mound of waste remains to arouse curiosity.

48 Lead Mining Tools E8

Great danger was faced by the lead miners in digging the ore, often working a ten hour shift from dawn. They may have walked long distances in all weathers to get to the mine and then there were the dangerous shafts and long passages to reach the ore face. No wonder that Daniel Defoe, writing in 1725, described the Wirksworth miner as: *'lean as a skeleton, pale as a corpse, his hair and beard deep black; what little flesh he had was lank and, as we thought, something of the colour of the lead itself'*. Boys too were employed down the mines, a small boot which would fit a boy of six has been found down a mine at Winster. The tools were crude, seen here is a wooden spade, a crusher and a candlestick. The wooden dish used for measuring the ore is a copy of the bronze Miners' Standard Dish kept in Moot Hall in Wirksworth.

Photo: courtesy of Derby Museum

30

49 The Bear Pit   D5

Water was always a great problem in the lead mines, and drains or 'soughs' were cut to the nearest river to 'unwater' them, to use the curious phraseology of the miners. The discharge from these drains occurs in many places in the valleys but is often passed unnoticed. An interesting example can be seen behind the shops on Cromford Hill just above the Market Place in the village. Here the Cromford Sough appears and disappears again deep in a walled enclosure known locally as the Bear Pit, there seems no explanation for this curious name. The sough was cut to drain the lead mines around Wirksworth, and here, augmented by other sources it was controlled by sluice gates before going on to power the cotton mills beside the Derwent. The figure gives the scale to the small tunnels, and equipped with waders and a helmet complete with a light he is removing silt from one of the tunnels. Not everyone's idea of an easy task, he is better equipped than the intrepid miners who cut these narrow drains long ago. Close by the Bear Pit stands the Old Village Lockup, owned by the Arkwright Society which has done so much to preserve all that is best in Cromford.

50 Cromford Sough Aqueduct D5

After the brief appearance in the Bear Pit seen in the previous illustration the waters of the Cromford Sough reappear in Mill Lane which they cross in the narrow cast-iron aqueduct seen here. It bears the date 1821 when it replaced one of wood. This water from the sough, augmented by the Bonsall Brook from the Via Gellia, originally powered a corn-mill before discharging into the Derwent. Later it powered Sir Richard Arkwright's cotton-mill and when the Cromford Canal was built in 1793 it helped to water that too. As the water from underground was always above freezing point the canal was usually navigable when others were perhaps icebound. Very gratifying to Arkwright as one of its instigators, but unfortunately he died before it opened. Today the aqueduct is an object of interest and curiosity to travellers along Mill Lane and to the thousands of visitors to the mill. The mill complex is an International Heritage Site where restoration work goes on, and here guided tours and shops and a restaurant make Cromford Mill an increasingly popular place to visit.

51 Leawood Pumphouse E6

The towpath of the Cromford Canal is a popular footpath from Cromford to Ambergate and where it crosses the River Derwent on Wigwell Aqueduct a pumping house attracts attention. It houses a beam engine which explains why it is so tall and narrow, and the engine, powered by two boilers from railway engines pumps water from the river into the canal. This topped up the water in the canal if water from the Cromford Sough (no. 49) diminished. The point where the water is drawn from the river can be seen from the aqueduct where a low arch becomes visible on the left bank when the river is low. Occasionally the engine house is open to the public and when working a great surge of water pours into the canal with each stroke of the engine. The tall chimney has an unusually large cap thought to be necessary to make it 'draw' in its position in the valley. If one wonders about the difficulty of constructing the overhanging cap in stone, the answer is that it is an iron casting. The pump house was built in about 1850 and today is in the care of the Derbyshire County Council's volunteer group, the Middleton Top Engine and Leawood Pump Group.

52 Wigwell Aqueduct E6

A walk beside the Cromford Canal is particularly rewarding in the wintertime when ice and snow give some beautiful effects. It also reveals that the Wigwell Aqueduct leaks. The canal was built by William Jessop and Benjamin Outram with Richard Arkwright as the main sponsor, and opened in 1793, a year after Arkwright's death. The aqueduct was rebuilt by Jessop about that time after the failure of the first one. This photograph was taken from the towpath of the Nightingale Canal built in 1802 to join the Cromford Canal here. This carried textiles from Peter Nightingale's mills at Lea Bridge and lead from his smelter a little higher up the valley (no. 47). The canals were taken over by the railways which closed Cromford Canal in 1944 but in 1947 it became the property of the

Derbyshire County Council. Today it is one of the county's finest amenities.

53 Butterley Tunnel   F6

The cutting of the Cromford Canal from the Derwent Valley to the Erewash Valley and its connection with the Erewash Canal in Golden Valley involved the digging of the Butterley Tunnel. Passing beneath Butterley in Ripley it is nearly 3,000 yards long, and being only nine feet wide with no towpath, boats were propelled by 'legging' i.e. men lying on the boat and 'walking' on the roof or sides of the tunnel. The tunnel was only partly brick-lined and twice it collapsed and after the second time in 1903 the tunnel was closed. The two insignificant entrances to the tunnel are now partly silted up and give no indication of the activities which went on beneath Ripley, for it passed directly beneath Butterley Ironworks. Two shafts connected the works with the canal and here wharfs received raw materials like iron ore and despatched the finished castings, and many tons of the cast iron wheels and flanged rails for the tramways (no. 16) were shipped from here. One of the county's industrial archaeological features and its strangest curiosity lies in the dark deep beneath the town of Ripley. Seen here is the Golden Valley entrance to the tunnel, and in the foreground the towpath which continued over the hill.

54 Milestone in a Fishpond D5

One wonders how many of the thousands of visitors who watch the fishes in the Fishpond at Matlock Bath notice the old milestone set in the wall just above the water level. Of a very simple type it records the distance to Chatsworth, Bakewell and Manchester and the date 1801. Invisible from the road today, this relic of more leisurely days was no doubt placed here to be preserved. Another example of an old milestone can be seen at Coldwall Bridge (no. 148).

55 A Column of Tuffa D5

Large deposits of tuffa have been 'growing' around Matlock Bath for millions of years, and this column of the sponge-looking but brittle stone standing in the Fishpond shows how it is formed. It is capped with a layer of moss and the water spray leaves a deposit of lime. When the moss dies it leaves holes in the solidified lime, a continuing process which means the column will 'grow' higher with time (nos. 56 and 57).

56 A Tuffa Grotto D5

In the late 18th century tuffa was extensively used as decoration in the gardens of the hotels in Matlock Bath, and this grotto was built over a spring in the gardens of the Royal Hotel which stood nearly opposite the Fishpond. Today this portion of the grounds is a car park and the grotto an object of curiosity to motorists. A similar example stands in the garden of the Peacock Hotel at Rowsley and in the churchyard nearby there is a rockery made of tuffa.

58 A Brave Policeman D5

An avenue which runs beside the River Derwent from Matlock Bridge in Matlock (no. 125) ends where the river makes a sharp bend to leave Hall Leys Park. Here was enacted a drama when a brave policeman lost his life in the river, and a metal plaque on a simple block of stone records the tragedy.

Erected by Public Subscription
To the Memory of Police Constable Arthur Wright, who lost his life by drowning whilst attempting to save the life of another. March 27th 1911.

It goes on to say that the stone was refurbished and rededicated on the 23rd March 1997 to commemorate the centenary of the Derbyshire Constabulary Mutual Welfare Fund. Close by is the children's playground and the park with its happy sports activities, and it is good to know that PC Wright is not forgotten in this quiet corner.

57 A Cable Tramway Shelter D5

Motorists circling the traffic island in Crown Square at Matlock will not have time to notice the large shelter in Hall Leys Park close by. Originally it was a tramway shelter standing on the same spot as the traffic island and serving a cable tramway which ran up Matlock Bank (seen below). The engine house still stands at the top on the corner of Rutland Street and Wellington Street. Its history makes interesting reading. In 1890 John Smith of Matlock suggested the idea and a company was formed, with George Newnes who founded the publishing firm, mainly financing it. Incidentally George Newnes was born at The Manse, Glenorchy Chapel in Cromford where his father was the Minister. It opened in 1893 and in 1898 he gave it to The Urban District Council. It must have been an exciting ride for the gradient averaged 1 in 5½, the fare being 2d up and 1d down. It closed in 1927.

59 Darley Dale Tombs   D5

These carvings around the sides of the table tombs near the porch in Darley Dale churchyard always attract interest. They date from the mid–18th century when the Huguenots, Protestant exiles from France, fled to England. The pictures of weaving frames carved on the sides indicate the trades they brought with them.

60 Darley Dale Coffins   D5

These sarcophagi lying beside the church in Darley Dale close by the tombs seen in the previous entry, are much older. The small one which contained the skeleton of a child, was unearthed from a foundation stone of the church and is thought perhaps to indicate a pagan custom. There is much of interest in Darley Dale church and churchyard.

61 Baslow Tombstone   D4

This very unusual and very substantial tombstone lies near the porch of Baslow Church. This solid block of stone is inscribed with the usual information about the person buried there in 1702, one Robin Stafford, with carvings in relief and imitation lifting rings at each end. One wonders why such a heavy block of stone, for there is no record of body snatching in Derbyshire, (no. 138) although it is believed to have taken place all over England.

62 A Coffin Lid Mystery   D4

The cross and two keys carved on this coffin lid preserved in Baslow church porch pose a question. Do the keys indicate that the person it commemorates was an official of some sort?

63 A Simple Tombstone   E9

This plain tomb is in striking contrast to
the elaborately carved examples shown in
the following entries, for it merely carries
the initials WB. It stands in the
churchyard at Foremark, and if you are
tempted to find the church (and 'find' is
the operative word, for it lies off the
Repton to Ingleby road in the Trent Valley
on a lane which ends at a farm) you will
be rewarded by a very interesting church
set in a quiet retreat. Following the
publication of the first Curiosity book
over twenty years ago readers have written
to say that the finding of these small and
less important examples has taken them
into little known corners of our county.
So it is with Foremark. The church has
remained unaltered since it was built in
1662 by Sir Francis Burdett of the hall
close by, using some material from a
previous chapel and also from a derelict
chapel at Ingleby. It has a three-decker
pulpit, box pews, a fine oak screen and
13th century font. The Communion rails
are by Derby's fine craftsman Robert
Bakewell as too are the large gates leading
into the hall grounds at the east end. The
arms of the Burdetts are depicted high
above on the church.

64 Why so Small ?   C5

As one would expect, Derbyshire has
some fine examples of carvings in alabaster
and this tomb chest in Youlgreave Church
always attracts admirers. It also arouses
curiosity because it is so small, being only
three and a half feet long. The figure is
that of Thomas Cockayne who died in
1488, and his head rests on a helmet with
a cock's head, the family crest. The
smallness of the figure has led to
speculation how young was Thomas when
he died, or did he die before his father, are
two suggestions which have been put
forward.

65 Brass Portraits D7

These fine brass portraits are fixed in the tomb of Sir Nicholas Kniveton and his wife which stands in Mugginton Church. His feet rest on a grey hound, but there is a curious interest in the helmet on which his head rests. The heraldic device includes a rare feature of which it is said there are only a few in the country. It shows a fox whose cub has been stolen pausing to look in a mirror thrown down by the thieves in which it thinks it sees its stolen cub. One wonders what heraldic significance this event has. One also wonders what is the story behind the 1,000 human skulls which were uncovered beneath the floor of the nave when alterations were made during the nineteenth century.

66 Anthony Bradshaw's Monument E7

This unusual monument in Duffield Church is to a remarkable man. He was Anthony Bradshaw and it records his two wives and twenty children and their figures are inscribed on the band across the middle of the monument. There should have been three more children but they were not born until after the monument was set up in 1600. Another curious fact is that Anthony's name appears as a rhyming acrostic on his panel and it is possible that he had composed it himself for he had already written a poem about Duffield Frith of which he was a deputy steward for a time.

67 Duffield's Old Yew Tree
   E7

Not surprisingly the gnarled remains of this old yew tree in Duffield churchyard has gathered to itself at least two legends. It is said that in the 4th century a recently converted army chaplain, after baptising converts in the River Derwent which runs beside the churchyard, noticed that they touched the yew tree. Recognising this as a pagan custom he baptised the tree too. A much later happening occurred when the tree was struck by lightning, and as it stands so close to the church it was claimed to have saved it from damage.

68 A Crinkle Crankle Wall
   D9

Visitors to the fine old church at Egginton may have their curiosity aroused by the crinkle crankle wall which borders the south side of the churchyard. Beyond it is a private garden, and these attractive features had a definite purpose for the curved alcoves were suntraps. The design was very strong, allowing them to be built much higher than the conventional type of wall. A similar wall runs beside the road at Hopton Hall.

69 A Church Stable   D7

Churches were sometimes built to serve more than one village as in the case of All Saints which stands in the fields about midway between Brailsford and Ednaston; in fact Brailsford is recorded in the Domesday Book as having '*half a church and half a priest*'. Travel in those days was by pony and trap, horseback or 'shank's pony', and sometimes a stable was built beside the church. This one at Brailsford stands by the churchyard gates and a tablet over the doorway once carried the date 1754 and the words '*This stable was erected at the expence of the parish*' but is now unreadable. The author does not know of a similar building in the county but a chapel and stable combined is seen in the next illustration. Brailsford Church can only be reached by road from the village or by footpath.

70 Chapel and Stable D6

This old chapel isolated in the fields over a mile south of Carsington village has quite a different reason for its loneliness from that of the church at Brailsford, for it dates from the 17th century when dissenters were compelled to build their chapels away from the villages. The chapel was built over the stable, and this recent photograph shows it has been enlarged and renovated and now used as the headquarters for the rangers who look after the amenities of the Carsington Reservoir which now fills the valley. The large stable door has been retained as too have the outside steps to the chapel, the roof of which has been raised slightly. It is good to see this historic link with the past preserved by the Severn Trent Water Authority. The reservoir was opened by Her Majesty the Queen in 1992 and the amenities there are well worth a visit, as seen in the next photograph.

71 The Kugal D6

One of Derbyshire's newest curiosities may be seen at Carsington Reservoir. This is The Kugal, a polished sphere of granite three feet in diameter which attracts the attention of adult and child alike. Made of Bavarian granite – Kugal is German for ball – it rests on a dished recess cut in a block of the same material, from which issues jets of water upon which it floats, rotating slowly. This is caused by two jets being at different pressures, and it can readily be turned by hand, even a child's. A notice informs us that it weighs over one ton and that the pressure of the water jets is only $17\frac{1}{2}$ pounds per square inch. One can only marvel at the power of hydraulics and wonder how the sphere was cut and polished. The complex of buildings at

Carsington includes a shop, an indoor and outdoor restaurant, and shops around the courtyard. There is a permanent exhibition which tells the story of water from the rainfall to the reservoir, from its purification to its issue from the tap. All this is shown graphically and in models with copious captions enjoyed by thousands of visitors every year.

72 An Ornate Cart Shed   C5

Gratton Grange Farm is situated beside the scenic road which links Elton with Youlgreave. It lies near Dale End about one mile west of Elton where Gratton Dale runs into the upper reaches of the River Bradford. An unusual cart shed at the farm arouses curiosity, for its carved stones bear the date 1853 and the initials WPT IT and one wonders why so ornate. The farm dates from the 17th century, but one wonders if these carved stones have any connection with two monastic settlements which stood nearby at Gratton and Smerrill.

73 Abbey House   F8

Visitors to the secluded little corner of the county known as Dale Abbey near Stanton by Dale may have wondered at the unusual cottage seen here. The tall east window of the abbey stands a short distance away and the massive stonework in the cottage is part of the abbey wall. The abbey was established in 1197 and flourished until its destruction at the Dissolution and today little remains except the east window although its site has been revealed and small relics preserved in a museum here. The quaint little church and a hermit's cave are not far away.

74 Smalley Church Doorway   F7

The little church of St. John the Baptist at Smalley was demolished in 1793 and rebuilt. On examination the clever spiral decoration in the south porch seems a little puzzling for the spiral changes direction at the capital on the left. This is caused by making the spirals on each side of the doorway symmetrical, and the only way to make the whole doorway symmetrical was to make the change at the top of the arch. One wonders if the problem was not seen until too late. Almost detached from the church is the delightful pagoda-type tower added in 1912. A stone engraved with a cross thought to be 800 years old reminds us of a previous church which stood here.

75 An Ornate Church Doorway D8

The small brick church at Trusley, about ten miles west of Derby, was built in 1713 by William Coke who lived at the nearby hall, as recorded in the parish register – '*Mem. 1713: opening of the new church when we had both vocal and instrumental musick the service read as at Cathedrals an Anthem very well performed Mr. Coke being one of the performers.*' Mr Coke was a regular churchgoer attending morning prayers before going hunting with his pack of harriers and returning in time for the evening service. The Cokes came here in 1418 and there are memorials to them in the church and the fine lead drainpipes are embossed with their coat of arms. These and the ornate doorway into the church seen here are said to have come from the hall when it was demolished. The coat of arms and initials of William Coke and his wife are on the altar-cover and of more than passing interest is the maiden's funeral garland said to have been carried at the funeral of virgins. This is a rare feature found only in two other Derbyshire churches, Matlock and Ashford-in-the-Water.

76 Doveridge Yew Tree B8

Second only to the famous yew tree in Darley Dale churchyard this one of seemingly multiple trunks standing in the churchyard at Doveridge has a girth of twenty feet. It stands between the churchyard gates and the church porch and generations of Doveridge folk have passed beneath its gnarled branches, including, according to tradition, the parson on his way to perform the marriage service of the ubiquitous Robin Hood at Tutbury.

77 A Lychgate Clock   C7

Clifton village lies about two miles from Ashbourne on the Sudbury road at the junction of the roads from Norbury and Hanging Bridge (no. 137).
Here stands the church; built in 1848 and designed by the Derby architect H. I. Stevens it is one of at least 40 Churches

designed by him in the county. Nikolaus Pevsner mentions 15 of these but does not include the village in his *Buildings of England*. One may assume that Stevens also designed the delightful lychgate here, for after all he included the ornamental chimney at Osmaston Manor (no. 32) when he designed that house. Although it is said he was not happy with his church at Shardlow, he could surely be pleased with this lychgate at Clifton with its steep roof and ornamental timbers, its bellcote and clock. The author cannot recall another similar in the county.

78 Shrovetide Football   C7

Although the famous Shrovetide Football game is still played at Ashbourne the goals have disappeared. These were two old water mills beside the Henmore Brook at Thurston and Clifton. The one at Clifton has been replaced by a rough stone column seen here with a plaque recording the game. It stands in a field beside the brook on the opposite side of the road to the derelict railway station on the Hanging Bridge road.

79 Shrovetide Football in Derby   E8

While Ashbourne was enjoying its Shrovetide football (no. 78) a similar activity was taking place in Derby, and this photograph of an actual ball used at that time puts a different complexion on the game. Although filled with cork it would be very heavy when wet and one can see why the game was also called 'Hug Ball'. Its size can be judged by the matchbox.

Photo: courtesy of Derby Museum.

The ball was thrown up by the Mayor from the safety of a window of the Guildhall in the Market Place, and the goals were the gallows at the top of Normanton Road and Nun's Mill. The teams were the parishes of All Saints and St. Peter and as at Ashbourne the more the merrier and with over 1,000 players, here too it was thought wise to board the windows. Efforts to stop the game in 1730 were unsuccessful as they were after a man was drowned in the Derwent in 1796. The game was discontinued about fifty years later when the militia and special constables had been called in.

80 Half a House   E8

Jacobean House, formerly Gisbourne Mansion, stands in the Wardwick, and is thought to be the first brick house to be built in Derby. The date over the doorway is either 1611 or 1677 but it is generally agreed that the former is correct. Becket Street runs beside it on the right and before this was built the house presented a long front to the Wardwick. It then had five gables and five attractive bays of two storeys, but two gables and two bays were destroyed and a third bay and gable were saved by rebuilding and 'turning' them into the new Becket Street. This portion of the Jacobean House is but a shadow of its former glory but still an attractive feature in the city. This photograph was taken over 50 years ago since when it has been put to various uses.

81 A Derby Tollhouse E8

Around the 18th century most of the roads into Derby were turnpiked, and at least three of the tollhouses still stand today, notably one on Burton Road and another on the Ashbourne Road near the junction with Windmill Lane. The third, shown here, is on Kedleston Road near the University. This was built in the mid-18th century and was in use until 1888 when all major roads became the responsibility of the County Councils. Taken in the days of the trolley busses it shows the typical bay window, an attractive feature which allowed approaching traffic to be seen in good time. Many tollhouses had similar classical features to those seen here and these reflected the tastes of the local gentry who comprised the Turnpike Trusts. These bodies decided the position of the tollhouses, and even had the power to close side roads where a diversion could be made to avoid the payment of tolls.

82 Midland Railway Crest
E8

This black and white photograph does not do justice to the colourful feature displayed in the large car park at Derby Midland Station. Whilst arousing curiosity in many motorists, railway buffs and local people will recognise it as the crest of the old Midland Railway. It shows the mythical bird the Wyvern and the whole pediment stood over the entrance to the station from 1892 when it was rebuilt until its demolition in 1988. In that year the modern frontage was built following the rebuilding of the rest of the station, and the pediment re-erected in its new position reminding us of Derby's important role in early railway history. This began in 1839 when the first train arrived from Nottingham at a temporary platform to great jubilation and church bell ringing. A few days later a regular service began. Later three more companies, the Midland Counties, Birmingham and Derby, and the North Midland arrived in Derby and by 1844 they were merged into the Midland Railway Company. The first station had been built in 1840, and a second one which followed was rebuilt in 1892 and carried the Wyvern pediment.

83 Friar Gate Bridge   E8

For 120 years the railway bridge has graced Friar Gate in Derby although when it was built in 1878 there was great opposition to it. Yet today, curiously, there would be similar opposition to its demolition. *The best street in the town hopelessly disfigured'* cried the Derby Mercury when work started in 1876, and there was acrimony in the Council Chamber when the project was supported by the Mayor who was also the railway's solicitor. Today the city is proud of '*the most decorative railway bridge ever built*' and of the firm of Andrew Handyside who built it. Handyside arrived in Derby in 1848 and the bridge shows the range of his work, from the huge arches of iron, each made of five castings, to the ornamental balustrades along the top to the spandrels which incorporate the Buck in the Park. There are two bridges, slightly out of line as they separate to embrace a central platform of the Great Northern line station. They also have two plaques with the date 1878, thought to be the date of the opening of the line. A thatched inn of at least 1751 called *The White Horse* which stood on the west side was demolished and Short Street opposite disappeared. The gentle slope of Georgian Friar Gate was 'dipped' to pass under the bridge and a number of plane trees donated by the townsfolk were sacrificed; now in maturity, those remaining enhance what is still considered Derby's finest street. The bridge stands on the proposed route of the inner ring road of St. Alkmund's Way, but should be retained as a tribute to Handyside's craftsmen.

84 Derby Tramways   E8

From Friargate Bridge the railway continued on arches as far as Lodge Lane and for some years they were used by small businesses until their demolition in the 1980s. The few arches next to the bridge were used as stables when horse-drawn trams were in use from 1880 to 1907 and although the lines have long ago disappeared from the city streets these still remain outside the stables as a record of this chapter in the history of the city's transport. This photograph taken from above the arches a few years ago shows the lines in their stone sets typical of the narrow streets like the George Yard and Thorntree Lane. The sets probably came from the granite quarries at Mount Sorrel just over the border in Leicestershire. Today this historic corner is becoming overgrown, but should be preserved as an example of the city's early transport system.

85   A Handyside Footbridge   E6

The firm of Andrew Handyside (no. 83) profited from the railway mania of the late 1840s and during the next 30 years played an important part in extending the railway age all over the world. They built bridges in Russia, Japan and Australia and other far flung places, and it is fitting that what is considered their most ornate should stand in Friar Gate in Derby. Derbyshire has what is perhaps their smallest bridge, this footbridge at Whatstandwell in the Derwent Valley. This crosses the railway line at the station, and the author remembers a small plaque with the date 1894 but this has since disappeared. The bridge gave access to the other platform and the path continues over the Cromford Canal for passengers who live on the Crich road. This branch line from Ambergate through Matlock was built in 1849 and older readers may remember the flowering borders beside the platforms when these local stations proudly competed with each other. Since 1984 the track has been reduced to one line, and the opposite platform, now overgrown with weeds, is closed.

86 Church Windows of Iron
E8

Travellers along Brook Street in Derby may not notice the delightful little cul-de-sac of St. John's Terrace where attractive houses look across Markeaton Brook to St. John's Church. They cannot fail to notice this unusual church with its corner turrets, but what is even more unusual and does pass unnoticed are the windows, for these are made of cast iron. They were made in Derby by the firm of Weatherhead and Glover in Britannia Foundry in Duke Street which also made the windows of the church at Shardlow. They were expert in ornamental cast-ironwork this being their main product but they ran only from 1818 to 1848 when they were taken over by Andrew Handyside (no. 83). Handyside continued window production and examples can be seen in mill cottages and mills around the county. Their catalogue of 1,500 different designs shows a delicacy which was difficult to emulate.

87 Elvaston's Golden Gates
F8

Derbyshire is rich in fine wrought-iron work made by Robert Bakewell the county's famous craftsman. It comes as a surprise to learn that the well-known Golden Gates in Elvaston Park came from abroad, brought here from Madrid, it is thought, by the 4th Earl of Harrington in 1879. They are brilliant in gold and blue. Elvaston Castle which is not really a castle, is situated in its park beside the road which runs from Borrowash on the Derby to Nottingham Road to the A6 London Road. Near this latter junction is the main gate to the castle and from which a long avenue (closed) leads to the Golden Gates which give entrance to the splendid gardens surrounding the castle. The gates can be reached from Elvaston Village situated on the road mentioned previously. Today the castle grounds are open to the public, for in 1970 Elvaston Park became England's first Country Park thus completing a county hat-trick, for in 1840 the Arboretum in Derby had become the first Municipal Park and the Peak District the first National Park in England in 1951.

88 An Italian Fountain E8

This ornamental fountain stands at the entrance to Derwent Park which lies between Duffield Road and Darley Grove on the northern side of Derby. It has had a varied life being brought from Italy by the Mundy family for their home at Markeaton Hall, and when the hall was demolished in the 1970s the fountain was sold. For many years it stood in a garden high above the river opposite High Tor in Matlock Bath, and today it has returned to Derby gracing the entrance to a public park not far from its first position in Markeaton Park.

89 Kedleston's Aspirations E8

Kedleston Hotel stands beside the Kedleston Road about three miles north of Derby. This fine building standing alone has an unusual origin and history, for it was not built for travellers along this old turnpike road to Ashbourne, but to accommodate visitors to a sulphur spring which stood in Kedleston Park opposite. It was built by one Lord Scarsdale of the Hall, and together with the iron spring at Quarndon nearby there were hopes of developing a spa here. The stables still stand behind the hotel but a large bowling green which stood across the road has gone. The water was sold in Derby as a substitute for malt liquor at a penny a quart, and an old print shows a donkey with water cans slung on panniers in Derby Market Place making a delivery. When the water ceased to flow in 1896 the hotel became Bath Farm, for the spring was housed in a delightful little building called Bath House. Today it is once again an hotel, shown on the Ordnance map as an inn about one mile from the Quarndon turn off.

90 The Bath House   E8

The Bath House still stands in Kedleston Park, admired by the golfers on the course of the Kedleston Golf Club which surrounds it.

91 Prior Overton's Tower   D9

The River Trent flows close by Willington, but originally it ran a mile away at the foot of the rise on which stands Repton Church, its route indicated by a string of oxbows. Here stands Prior Overton's Tower, attached to a building of Repton School on the edge of the old water course. It was built by Prior John Overton in the 15th century, a fine

example of Gothic brickwork with turrets and battlements. It can be seen from the bridge over the old water course which carries the road into Repton Village. Repton is the most historical and picturesque spot in south Derbyshire and perhaps in the whole county, with its cross and Norman entrance into the famous school in the centre to the church and Saxon crypt close by.

92 In Netherseal Village   D11

The village of Netherseal lies close to the borders of Leicestershire, Warwickshire and Staffordshire in the far south of Derbyshire. Here pedestrians cannot fail to notice the curious shaping of the rock at the base of a high wall. The village is built on rock and it was once thought that the name 'seal' came from the word 'rock' but this has now been discounted. The author could not find anyone who could explain how the rock had been worn in this way, and readers may have their own theories. The wall encloses the grounds of Netherseal Hall demolished in 1930. This was the home of the Gresleys whose name lives on in Church Gresley and Castle Gresley, and railway buffs may like to visit the grave of Sir Nigel Gresley who lies among the family graves not far away.

93 Monks' Bridge D9

From its source high in Axe Edge down to its confluence with the Trent at Newton Solney, the River Dove is crossed by many lovely bridges and perhaps the oldest stands near Egginton. This is Monks' Bridge said to have been built by the monks of Burton Abbey in the 15th century. It is now in retirement, superseded by a new concrete bridge seen here through the arches.

94 Brindley's Aqueduct D9

A few yards downstream from Monks' Bridge the Dove is crossed again, this time by a low aqueduct built by the canal pioneer James Brindley in 1777 to carry his Trent and Mersey Canal. There are 12 arches probably to make sure it could accommodate flood waters. A great achievement in its day and very busy in its heyday it is now admired by the users of pleasure craft on the canal who also get a nice view of Monks' Bridge.

95 An Elegant Footbridge B8

The village of Doveridge may be thought to take its name from the ridge over the Dove, but in fact it comes from the Roman crossing of Dove Bridge. This has been superseded by a modern concrete span nearby, but a little further down the river there is an elegant suspension bridge built on a footpath. The road past the church in Doveridge (no. 76) ends at the bridge where the footpath continues across the fields to the modern bridge upstream. One wonders why a footpath merits such a splendid footbridge.

96 A well-preserved Cider Mill C8

Although one frequently sees cider mills preserved on the village greens of the orchard counties of Hereford and Worcestershire, this is the only example known to the author in Derbyshire. It stands at Sapperton Manor near Boyleston in south Derbyshire and is a well-preserved example, only the pole to which the horse was harnessed is missing. I am indebted to the Prince family who allowed me to photograph it, and have given me the following information. Michael Prince tells me that it came from his uncle's farm at Eaton Dovedale near Doveridge about 60 years ago. It stood in an orchard there but there is no record or memory of it being used. It is good to see it in perfect condition and well looked after, perhaps unique in the county.

55

97 Bee Boles   E4

Until sugar was introduced into this country honey was the universal sweetener. Beehives made of straw called skeps were a common sight, and to protect them from the weather they were housed in 'bee boles' which were recesses in the garden walls or walls of the house. In the mid-1800s the wooden hive with its moveable frame was introduced, and as this could be moved around the garden or orchard or even onto the moors, it was a great advance. Today many of these 'bee boles' remain, some dating from the 15th century, but the author has not been able to trace any more in Derbyshire other than those pictured here. These fine examples stand in the garden of Stud Farm Cottage in Walton on the southern outskirts of Chesterfield. They are built beneath the terrace fronting the house and were photographed several years ago when the house was being restored, and it is good to see these fascinating features carefully retained. The house stands near the top of Bacon Lane where it joins the Matlock to Chesterfield road at a very busy traffic island.

98 Hangman's Stone   E9

This unimpressive stone lying beside a footpath near Ticknall in South Derbyshire is shown on old Ordnance Maps as Hangman's Stone. It is a boundary stone from the days when each district was responsible for its own law and order and could not encroach on its neighbour. The story goes that a thief with a sheep on his back held by a rope round his shoulders rested the sheep on the stone. When the sheep slipped off the back of the stone he was hanged. The story is almost certainly apocryphal, for there are other Hangman's Stones with a similar tale. The stone can be found where two footpaths cross on the hill south of Bendalls Farm near Foremark Reservoir. The farm is shown on the Landranger Map.

99 Gibbet Stone E5

This stone lying beside the road at a junction about one mile north-east of Dethick Church is known locally as the Gibbet Stone. The square hole is thought to be the socket for the gibbet post but there seems no record of this. It looks like a millstone, and in fact a mill once stood beside the Lea Brook not far away. Perhaps the underneath of the stone would give a clue to its origin. Dethick, a church and three farms, is famous as the birthplace of Antony Babington of the Babington Plot designed to overthrow Queen Elizabeth I and put Mary Queen of Scots on the throne. Dethick lies about two miles east of Cromford.

100 An Ash House D4

This small building stands alone in a field beside the road which crosses the hills between Baslow and Hassop. It has always been known as the Ash House and thought to have been built for storing potash used in the making of glass. Bracken and glassweed etc, were burnt and the resultant potash pressed into blocks and stored here. The author has seen similar ash houses on farms on Dartmoor in Devon, but there the ash was spread on the fields as a fertiliser. Whatever the purpose of this little building and readers may have their own ideas, it arouses curiosity and is bound to gather to itself local legends. An interesting tale once told in Baslow is of an old shepherd who lived here and hid his money in the roof. A thief who climbed on the roof fell through, killing himself, the shepherd and his dog. The road is still a lonely one, and 'tis said that whistling heard upon these hills in the dusk is that of the shepherd calling for his old friend.

101 England's First Cheese Factory C8

It was an American, Cornelius Schermerhorn who opened the first cheese factory in England, and although a cheese had been made at a factory in Derby a month earlier, the factory had not been built for that purpose. This first cheese factory seen here was opened at Longford in 1870 and within a few years many more were opened in the county. The small plaque seen on the board above the platform records its place in history.

102 Cottage Cheese Press E5

Many cottages and farms had their cheese presses and this complete example stands outside a cottage in Kelstedge near Ashover. Portions of presses may be found around the county used as building materials or sometimes built into walls for preservation, and it is interesting to look out for them. The base of a press stands beside the road near Longnor just over the border in Staffordshire well within the Peak District. It is used as a stand for milk churns from a farm. The large stone block of a press is built into a farm building opposite the *Knockerdown* public house near Hognaston.

103 A Pair of Cheese Presses E9

Although one sometimes finds a single cheese press in our villages or farms, this is the only pair the author has found in Derbyshire. They stand close by the Norman Tympanum at St. Brides Farm near Melbourne (no. 165). The base of the press near Longnor mentioned in the previous entry was also a double press.

seedling in the roof gutter of the inn and ended its days in the garden *(below, left)*. At the eastern end of the street stands the modern cross erected to Edward VIII who was never crowned. Here visitors will be intrigued by Jawbone Lane. Many years ago the author photographed an arch formed by the jawbone of a whale which stood at the entrance to King's Newton House, placed there by the Chantrill family who once lived there. Decayed, it was taken down in the 50s. A recent visit shows that Jawbone Lane is complete again, for Mr Ron Stafford, long a resident there and a keen local historian, heard of a whale being washed ashore on an island near Skye in Scotland and had the jawbone brought to Derbyshire where it now stands outside his home *(below)*.

104 Whale's Jawbone F9

The delightful main street of King's Newton near Melbourne in south Derbyshire is full of interest. At the western end *The Packhorse Inn* served the packhorse track which still winds its way down to the river at Swarkestone Bridge. A little way along the street, the Hall, one time home of the Hardinges, faces the *Hardinge Arms* where the famous Newton Wonder apple originated. It began as a

105 Bob, Bold, Mona and Nell A4

This impressive decorated column standing seven feet high is situated in a garden at Burbage near Buxton. It is thought to have been erected by a farmer in memory of his dogs Bob, Bold, Mona and Nell and their names are carved on its sides. It is also thought to have been put up by a Macclesfield silk manufacturer who had a shooting lodge here.

106 A Pets' Cemetery F9

Many of the great houses had their pets buried in a secluded corner of the grounds and this one at Melbourne Hall is often missed by visitors. It is situated in the far southern corner of the gardens where the boundary wall forms a curve, and here are several graves with their tablets set in the wall.

107 Fence-cum-Stile C7

There are numerous types of stiles in Derbyshire, and like that shown in no. 151, the one shown here is also probably unique in the county. It is however, quite different from the stone squeeze type common in the Peak, being an ingenious example of the joiner's craft giving no indication of its purpose as one approaches. Only the walker will find it for it stands on a footpath which crosses the hills from Clifton (nos. 77 and 78) south of Ashbourne to the neighbouring village of Snelston. Here it enters Snelston Park close by the copse of monkey puzzle trees shown in the next photograph, and crosses a stream which feeds the lake below and climbs to emerge in a road. Here a right turn takes one past the church and hall lodge and into the very pleasant village.

108 Monkey Puzzle Trees C7

The Monkey Puzzle tree was very popular in Victorian times and one is occasionally seen in a front garden today, but to see a copse of them is very rare. This group can be seen near the stile shown in the previous photograph and like that is also unique in the county and perhaps in the whole country. The tree is the Chile Pine which was introduced into England by Sir Joseph Banks whose Derbyshire home was Overton Hall near Ashover. This famous naturalist brought back many different seeds from his world journey with Captain Cook and was knighted and made President of the Royal Society. He gave the seedlings of the Chile Pine to Kew gardens in 1795. The vicious spines on its leaves gave rise to the comment that to climb it *would be a puzzle to a monkey* and the name has continued since first coined in 1844.

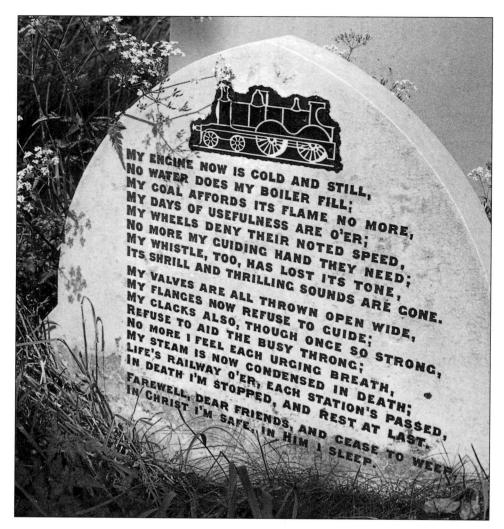

MY ENGINE NOW IS COLD AND STILL,
NO WATER DOES MY BOILER FILL;
MY COAL AFFORDS ITS FLAME NO MORE,
MY DAYS OF USEFULNESS ARE O'ER;
MY WHEELS DENY THEIR NOTED SPEED,
NO MORE MY GUIDING HAND THEY NEED;
MY WHISTLE, TOO, HAS LOST ITS TONE,
ITS SHRILL AND THRILLING SOUNDS ARE GONE.
MY VALVES ARE ALL THROWN OPEN WIDE,
MY FLANGES NOW REFUSE TO GUIDE,
MY CLACKS ALSO, THOUGH ONCE SO STRONG,
REFUSE TO AID THE BUSY THRONG;
NO MORE I FEEL EACH URGING BREATH;
MY STEAM IS NOW CONDENSED IN DEATH;
LIFE'S RAILWAY O'ER, EACH STATION'S PASSED,
IN DEATH I'M STOPPED, AND REST AT LAST.
FAREWELL, DEAR FRIENDS, AND CEASE TO WEEP,
IN CHRIST I'M SAFE, IN HIM I SLEEP.

109 A Railwayman's Grave
E8

This stone in Nottingham Road Cemetery in Derby always arouses curiosity. It stands beside the path which runs parallel with the Nottingham Road. Turn right on entering the Cemetery. It stands at the foot of the grave of Abel Boden, his wife and three daughters and bears the date 19th September 1921. On reading the stone one wonders if Abel had been a railwayman, for the verse is almost identical to one in memory of Thomas Scaife, an engineer on the Midland and Gloucester Railway who was killed by the explosion of an engine boiler in Bromsgrove Station in November 1840. This stone in Derby makes interesting reading, although a recent visit shows it badly stained and difficult to read, standing as it does at the foot of a large tree. The headstone records that Abel and his wife died on the same day, a curious and poignant fact.

110 A Comedian's Tragic End   A4

The ancient chapel of St Anne stands not far from the Market Place in Buxton and here in the graveyard is an unusual grave. It is that of John Kane, an 18th century comedian who died in agony after eating hemlock roots mistaking them for horse-radish. His grave lies at the eastern end of the churchyard, and the headstone is at the foot of the grave thus facing the opposite way to all the others.

111 A Quaker Graveyard A3

Ford Hall is situated on the outskirts of Chapel-en-le-Frith about two miles out on the A625 Castleton Road. Close by the hall drive a small enclosure is easily missed. A small gateway gives access and on one gatepost are carved the words Friends Burial Ground and the date 1668 while within the enclosure are six gravestones one with the date 1671. There are few Quaker burial grounds in the county, but the author recalls another behind a Friends' Meeting House in Monyash village.

112 A Grim Reminder   C7

Visitors to the ancient market town of Ashbourne usually find their way to the lovely and historical church at the end of Church Street. The fine wrought-iron gates into the churchyard are thought to be the the work of the county's craftsman Robert Bakewell (no. 63) and the Heritage Lottery Fund has given a grant of £15,900 towards their restoration. What may not be noticed are the tall gateposts with the huge capping stones resting on stone skulls reminding us of our certain mortality.

113 An Eminent Quill Driver D6

When passing through a churchyard few can resist pausing to read the words on the tombstones, the sharing of sorrow with the parents at the loss of a child, or a chuckle with some boisterous wit whose character lives on in a few well chosen words. A favourite with the author is the tablet fixed on a buttress beside the west doorway of Wirksworth Church. It is to Philip Shallcross, an eminent quill driver to the town, in the 18th century, and the tablet records his invincible attachment to cats and dogs and his unbounded benevolence to them as well as towards his fellow creatures. A short verse on the tablet ends with the line *'That much esteemed he lived and much regretted fell'* a sentiment of which I feel sure he was worthy.

114 A Famous Author C6

Nat Gould, famous author of the late 1800s is in strange contrast to the gentle figure of Philip Shallcross featured in the previous entry. Although born of farming stock in the Hartington and Bradbourne area, Nat Gould was born in Manchester and sent to work on his uncle's farm in

Bradbourne, where he grew to love the Derbyshire countryside. This was the setting for many of his novels with Bradbourne as his 'Millbourne'.

He took a job as a journalist in Newark and attended race meetings in neighbouring towns, astounding everyone with his ability to pick the winners. He moved on to Australia where he became famous as a tipster and began to write short stories and racing novels – 130 in all with a total of 25 million sold. He came back to England in 1895 to walk the hills and dales of his beloved Derbyshire declaring *'I have travelled in many lands but have never seen a more beautiful place'*. He never lost touch with his home and said *'When my brain and body require rest I flee to these dear old hills of home'*. He lies beneath this simple cross near the gates of Bradbourne churchyard.

115 A Chantry Masterpiece
B6

Ilam Village, just over the border in Staffordshire, is probably the loveliest corner in the Peak District; the gateway to Dovedale and the Manifold Valley. Close by the hall is the village church with Saxon relics to prove its origin and a wonderful piece of sculpture by Sir Francis Chantry. Here David Watts of the hall is seen with his grieving daughter and her children in this deathbed scene, one of his finest works. It lies in an octagonal chapel Chantry designed for it. He was born in 1871 in Norton near Sheffield when that village was still in Derbyshire.

116 Ilam Hall   B6

In this view from the terrace at Ilam Hall the entrance to Dovedale is seen beside Thorpe Cloud which from here is seen to be wedge-shaped. The decorative pedestals on the terrace are actually chimneys, placed here when a portion of the hall was demolished. In the early 1930s the hall and its surroundings which comprise Ilam Estate Country Park, were bought by Sir Robert McDougall and presented to the National Trust. The Hall is now a Youth Hostel and there is an information centre and shop.

117 An Elegant Toilet   B6

There is much to interest and arouse the curiosity in Ilam. Close by the Hall this tall elegant building has the appearance of a gazebo although the small openings at the top would restrict the viewing. No doubt it was built with the Hall in the 19th century as a delightful garden feature. Close inspection today reveals it has been converted into a toilet, surely the most attractive in the county!

118 A Cottage Lintel   B6

Below Ilam Hall the River Manifold sweeps round a curve with a great amphitheatre of woods in an area called Paradise. Here beside the footpath is preserved a badly worn Saxon Cross rescued from a cottage when the village was rebuilt by Jesse Watts Russell. It had served as a lintel over a window. There are the remains of two Saxon Crosses in the churchyard, and it is good to see this one saved too.

119 The Capricious Manifold   B6

The habit of the River Manifold of disappearing below ground in dry weather has a curious effect in the winter. There are several 'sinks' and in this one near Darfur Crags the water has disappeared after freezing over, leaving the ice suspended, a curious phenomenon.

120 In Lathkill Dale C4

The River Lathkill, like the Manifold seen in the previous entry, flows part of its course below ground in dry weather. In wet seasons it pours from this cave near the head of the dale. The cave is extensive with several large caverns, and only the experienced should venture into such caves for any distance. The author with this party went in a short distance and recorded the fact by leaving a small brass plate stamped with their names and the date 1937 in a crevice in the rock. The figures in the photograph are:

Frank Rodgers, Jack Waite, Jack Hobday and Alf Woodall

121 A Remarkable Fence D7

This attractive fence is made with the staves of old barrels, the curve and shape of each stave making a very unusual design. They are of oak, and having been pickled for many years, probably in beer, should be very durable. It makes a change from barrels converted into garden tubs. The fence can be seen at Fiddlers Green near Brailsford and was thought to be unique, except there is another one a little further down the road!

122 A Fence of Rollers E3

These two old stone rollers have been put to good use as a fence at Cartledge Hall in Holmesfield and at the same time preserving them as a curiosity. The village of Holmesfield lies north west of Chesterfield.

123 A Very Durable Fence D3

Nothing could be more durable than a fence made of gritstone slabs as seen here fronting modern bungalows at Froggatt in the upper Derwent Valley. A not uncommon sight they probably came from the moors above.

124 An Unusual Type of Weir D5

This mill dam crosses the River Derwent at Cromford Mill and is very unusual as it curves downstream. When this photograph was published in a national magazine with a worldwide circulation it aroused great interest and several letters were received by the author. One from Canada pointed out that beavers always curved their dams downstream in this way, which, the writer said, *'must prove something'*.

125 Lost Millstones   D5

Visitors to Matlock often pause on the bridge over the River Derwent admiring the view of Riber Castle. One wonders how many notice the millstones lying in the river below and wonder how and when they got there.

126 Peeping Tom   C2

When the Ladybower Reservoir was built in the upper Derwent Valley, Derwent Hall was demolished and the site of Derwent Woodlands village submerged. Peeping Tom, seen here looking over the garden wall of the Hall, may now be seen in the Information Centre at the Derwent Reservoir higher up the valley.

127 A House at Whatstandwell   E6

Surely no more unusual site for a house can be found than this one at Whatstandwell. As can be seen here it stands directly over a tunnel through which all the trains to Matlock pass. This photograph was taken from the platform of the station close by the Handyside footbridge (no. 85). The towpath of the now derelict Cromford Canal runs beside the house and below it the busy A6 road crosses the well-known Whatstandwell Bridge (no. 128).

128 Whatstandwell   E6

There is often speculation about the origin of the name Whatstandwell, a village between Belper and Cromford in the Derwent Valley. About 150 years ago it was on record as *'Hot Standwell'* while old maps once showed it as *'Hotstandwell'*. It has even been claimed as *'Wilt Stand Well'* for here the River Derwent is crossed by Whatstandwell Bridge. The matter is settled by a charter of 1393 of Dale Abbey who owned this district which states that *'Agreement between Thomas Abbot, of Darley and the Convent, and John de Stepul, reciting that John intends*

to construct at his own cost a bridge over the Derwent next the house which Walter Stonewell had held of the Convent where no bridge had ever been constructed'. In the 1800s a turnpike road between Crich and Wirksworth crossed the valley here, and when the valley road between Belper and Cromford was built, now the very busy A6, this created a very nasty S bend. Here drivers have to slow down, giving them time to puzzle over the name which greets them on their approach. *The Derwent Hotel* seen in the photograph has been popular since the days of the stagecoach and still keeps its mounting block.

129 A Once Busy Spot   A4

Many of the old coach roads which crossed the Derbyshire hills are today green tracks trodden only by sheep or the rambler. One of the most delightful crosses the moors between Buxton and Macclesfield, crossing the top of the Goyt Valley and passing the *Cat and Fiddle Inn*. Here it is seen at Burbage near Buxton where it passes over the derelict High Peak Railway. Now silent, this spot once echoed to the sound of a train entering Burbage tunnel or of a coach straining up the hill. The stone commemorating the four dogs stands in a cottage garden not far away (no. 105).

130 Solomon's Temple   A4

Solomon's Temple stands high on Grin Low above Buxton with extended views over the town and surrounding hills. It was built in 1895 and replaced a simple structure said to have been built by a farmer named Solomon Mycock on the site of a prehistoric burial mound called Grin Low Barrow. Like so many of these towers, it was said to have been built to provide work for the unemployed and standing on the 1,000 contour line is seen from afar. It has a viewing platform reached by a spiral staircase. There is a car park off the nearby Grin Low Road, or it can be reached by a long but very pleasant footpath through the Buxton Country Park mentioned in the next entry. It is shown on the Landranger Ordnance Map.

131 Poole's Cavern   A4

Buxton Country Park is a wooded and beautiful area of 100 acres reclaimed from the dereliction left from lime burning and quarrying (next entry). In 1820 it was developed into a mixed woodland and extends from Solomon's Temple down to the outskirts of Buxton and here lies Poole's Cavern which has taken its name from a robber of the 15th century who stored his ill–gotten gains there. It extends 700 yards into the hillside with the usual strange rock formations and stalactites and stalagmites. One column with the name Mary Queen of Scots Pillar commemorates a visit of the ill–fated Queen when in the custody of the Earl of Shrewsbury. A spring which passes through the cave is said to be the source of the River Wye but it disappears to reappear at Burbage and continue down Serpentine Walks. This photograph was taken many years ago, and today there is a shop, visitor centre and video show together with a display of items found in the cavern. Poole's Cavern is shown on the Landranger Ordnance Map.

132 Modern Troglodytes
A4/B3

Nearly two centuries ago the large hillocks of waste from the lime kilns around Buxton were converted into dwellings by kiln and quarry workers. Locally called Ash Hillocks, these mounds of 'esse' became solid on the surface through the years, and were hollowed out to form caves with doors and windows. They were claimed to be warm in the winter and cool in the summer but could hardly be called desirable residences, yet it is recorded that in 1811 over a hundred families of lime workers lived in them. They were variously described as rabbit warrens and ant hills where animals continued to graze. Living so close to the wealthy and often famous visitors, they too had their own hierarchy with knights and barons, dukes and duchesses. The photograph on the r74 ight was taken about fifty years ago on the slopes of Grin Low mentioned in no.130 and the second at Doveholes which lies astride the A624 about three miles north of Buxton. These were said to have been inhabited until the end of the 1800s since when they have gradually collapsed as seen here in 1991. Readers walking in the Buxton area may still find evidence of these latter-day cave dwellers.

133 Peak Forest Church B3

Only a few churches are dedicated to the memory of King Charles the Martyr. This one stands in Peak Forest, a lonely village lying astride the busy A63 north-east of Buxton. What brings the curious here is the history of the chapel which stood here originally. This was built in 1667 by the then Countess of Devonshire as a private chapel and was outside episcopal jurisdiction and had the authority to conduct runaway marriages as at Gretna Green, the couples coming from far and wide. In its heyday more than one marriage a week took place here, earning the minister the goodly sum of £100 per year. The vicar, who had the grand title of *'The Principal Officer and Judge in Spiritualities in the Peculiar Court of Peak Forest'* ended the practice in 1804. When the chapel was demolished the Devonshires built the present church in 1877.

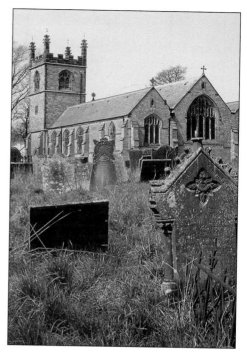

134 Peak Forest Mill B3

Place names can be very misleading in the Peak District, notably the 'lows' like Arbor Low and Grin Low which indicate burial mounds and are invariably situated on hilltops. There are few trees on the hills around Peak Forest, although the old meaning of the word forest did not mean wooded and the visitor may be greeted by the rooks which frequent the trees around the churchyard. Here a minor road leaves the main road and runs beside the churchyard to end at the site of the old water mill, although a footpath continues down Dam Dale and others to Millers Dale. The mill in Peak Dale has been modernised and in the foreground are two sheep-dipping enclosures, the water culverted to them from under the dried dam above. Damside Farm nearby has a collection of farm relics including an old plough and a broken quern.

135 Five Wells Tomb B4

The hills of Derbyshire are rich in prehistoric remains, notably Arbor Low and the burial mounds on Minninglow Hill. Second only to Minninglow is Five Wells on Taddington Moor which at a height of 1,400 feet above sea level is the highest megalithic tomb in England. It takes its name from five springs which rise close by. The earth mound which covered the chambers has gone as too have the capping stones. The chambers were approached by passages now open and within the chambers were found implements and skeletons. The tumulus lies on private land and I am indebted to the farmer of Five Wells Farm for his courtesy and permission to photograph it. A footpath from Taddington to

Chelmorton passes the farm, running down the road to it. Shown on the Landranger Ordnance map as a Chambered Cairn.

136 Strip Fields at Chelmorton B4

The church at Chelmorton is the highest parish church above sea level in Derbyshire and also claimed as the highest in England. Beyond the church are seen examples of the narrow strip fields which climb the hill behind each farm and which were originally open but are now enclosed. There are many interesting facts about the village from the church porch full of ancient carved stones to the curiously named Illy Willy Water, a spring which once ran openly beside the village street. Curiosity is aroused by Coals Lane, a name which reminds us that coal from the mines in the Dane Valley above Buxton once passed through the village. The village has managed to keep its stone telephone box.

137 Hanging Bridge   C7

Hanging Bridge crosses the River Dove at the bottom of Swinscoe Hill a few miles west of Ashbourne. Its name often arouses curiosity and it has been suggested that it comes from the time when criminals of Derbyshire and Staffordshire were hanged near this spot. There seems no record of this but it may have some credence for a Gallows Tree Lane drops straight down to the bridge from Upper Mayfield to cross squarely over the river. When the road was turnpiked in 1786 it avoided Upper Mayfield by coming obliquely down Swinscoe Hill to make a sharp bend over the bridge. This sharp turn at the bottom of a very steep hill has been the scene of many accidents. A newspaper report of 1830 records that the Manchester to London stagecoach crashed into pieces here but strangely does not mention any casualties. It does however state that the coach had called at many inns as it was New Year's Day! In this photograph are seen the arches of the old packhorse bridge, but long before this the Roman Hereward Street must have crossed the river hereabouts on the route between Rocester and Chesterfield.

138 Foiling the Body Snatchers   D1

Although there seems no evidence of Resurrection men or body snatchers in Derbyshire (no. 61) this gruesome activity was certainly feared in the village of Bradfield on the moors above Sheffield. It lies within the Peak District National Park, and beside the churchyard gates stands the Watch House, a curious building erected to prevent thieves from stealing the bodies of the newly buried. It was built by the Feoffees family and the two central windows were blocked during the time of the hated window tax. The author has taken photographs of other watch houses around Edinburgh also mortsafes which were anchored to the ground. The passing of the Anatomy Act in 1832 ended the need for these grim safeguards.

Mortsafes in Logierait Churchyard, Scotland

139 Boot's Folly D2

Seen from afar this tower on the edge of Bradfield Moor stands high above Strines Reservoir to the south of Bradfield Village. It is 50 feet high and there is a room about half way up, steps continuing to the top. It is thought the room may have been used as an observatory. The tower was built in 1927 by a local business man, Charles Boot who lived at Bent House a short distance away. The stone was gathered from round about and the date stone above the doorway was saved from the ruins of Nether Hoyle Farm which stood nearby. There seems no reason for the tower's erection, but it has been suggested that it was built to provide

work for the unemployed, a reason often given for the building of such isolated towers. If it is true in this case, it seems unkind to call it Boot's Folly as it has been nicknamed. It is shown on the Landranger Ordnance Map.

140 From Stable to Hospital A4

The Crescent and the Devonshire Royal Hospital designed by John Carr of York for the Duke of Devonshire have graced Buxton since 1790. The building seen here was originally built as stables to serve The Crescent but the coming of the railway soon reduced their use. In 1859 part of the stables was unused and then in 1878, the entire building was passed over by the 7th Duke to the Buxton Bath Charity. In 1881 the central courtyard was roofed over creating what was then the largest dome in Europe. These two splendid buildings cost the Duke £120,000, the profit, it is said, from one year at his copper mines in the Manifold Valley.

141 A Colourful Gateway G3

Standing beside the main road which runs through Barlborough in the north-east of the county, this unusual gateway excites interest. The small glazed tiles are of bright colours and, together with the Greek letters, are curiously foreign to Derbyshire. It was built by a member of the Rodes family of Barlborough Hall in memory of a lady of the house, Felicity de Rodes, and is the entrance to a small Garden of Remembrance to the fallen of the past two wars.

143 Russett Well C2

This huge spring at Castleton has an unfailing supply of water for it is said to never give less than 1,000 gallons a minute and ten times that amount in wet weather. Tests have shown that it drains high ground around Sparrow Pits and off Rushup Edge, and it is suggested that the name may be a corruption of Rushup. In its journey the water passes through the Speedwell Mine near the Winnats and when it emerges at Castleton its temperature is always 42 degrees Fahrenheit. The spring is situated in a cottage garden besides Peak Water where it emerges from Peak Cavern and permission to view is usually given by the owner.

142 A Chapel at Matlock Bath D5

The famous Lord Byron, John Ruskin and others have sung the praises of Matlock Bath, some having likened it to Switzerland. This chapel standing high on Masson Hill across the Derwent from High Tor, has fitted into that picture for just over a century. This is St. John the Baptist, designed by Sir Guy Dawber and built in 1897. It is strange that it was built over a well, the arch of which can be seen beyond the figure on the left. The oriel window and bell turret enhance this little chapel which fits perfectly into its dramatic setting.

144 An Ebbing and Flowing Well   B3

About six miles away across the hills from Castleton, the Ebbing and Flowing Well in Barmoor Clough is far less impressive in appearance and performance than Russett Well. In contrast to that copious flow, this feature is easily missed for its output is very intermittent, hence its name, and there is usually only a wet area around a depression. This is one of the two springs with the same name in the Peak District and there has been conjecture which is the one in the Seven Wonders of the Peak, which seems to indicate that it gave a much more dramatic performance years ago than it does today. It may be seen just over the wall in a field opposite Bennetston Hall in Barmoor Clough near Chapel en le Frith. Shown on the Landranger Ordnance Map.

145 A Cryptic Message   D8

The first written reference to the sundial may be found in the Bible, - 'the sundial of Ahas' in Isaiah 38:8 - and many different methods of telling the time by the sun have been devised since those distant days. Derbyshire has examples of various types from the simple to the elaborate and the messages they carry are equally varied, from the usual 'I only count the sunny hours' to 'Tempus Fugit' reminding us that time flies. A more cryptic message is seen on the dial on the church close by Kedleston Hall for it carries the words 'Wee Shall', leaving us to complete the 'Die All' (dial). The unusual shape of the style which casts the shadow is necessary as the dial is fixed to the east face of the church and catches only the early sun, and as can be seen only the hours six to ten are shown. Its odd location is said to be that it was intended for the benefit(?) of the domestic staff of the Hall. This attractive dial is almost certainly the only one of its type in the county and probably in the whole country.

146 A Farm Sundial   D7

Churches, the big houses and market
places all had their sundials, but it is
unusual to find one on a farm, and this
very attractive example gives its name to
Sundial Farm at Brailsford near Derby. It
is fixed on a bracket projecting from a
building so that it faces south, showing
that care has been taken to make it
accurate. The long shadow which
continues off the dial onto the brickwork
is cast by the conventional type of style
and indicates that the photograph was
taken in the late afternoon. One wonders
why this fine decorative feature should be
fixed on a farm building, and is there
another Sundial Farm?

147 Why so Tall ?   C6

A sundial tops this pedestal in the
churchyard at Thorpe north of Ashbourne,
and as it is too high to be read by
pedestrians one may assume it was
designed for horse riders. As it stands
among the gravestones one must also
assume it is not in its original position.
Furthermore the gnomon which casts the
shadow is set at an angle of 35 degrees
exactly whereas Thorpe stands on altitude
35 degrees three seconds. The design of
the sundial is an exact science and this one
was made by Whitehurst and it is unlikely
that this famous Derby clockmaker would
make such a mistake, perhaps these three
angle seconds would make little difference.
However it is not *in situ* and one wonders
where it stood originally.   The Ashbourne
to Buxton turnpike road once passed
through Mappleton and past Thorpe and
the Ashbourne to Blythe Marsh in
Staffordshire turnpike turned off here to
pass the church and cross the River Dove
at Coldwall Bridge. Could it be that the
sundial had a connection with these old
coach roads? Pure speculation but one can
imagine the coachman stopping to look
down on this sundial.

148 A Lonely Milestone C6

The importance of the road over Coldwall Bridge referred to in the previous entry is evidenced by this milepost which stands on the approach to the bridge. Simple guidestones which gave no mileage were made compulsory in 1702, but the Turnpike Acts of 1766 and 1773 which brought tollroads and tollhouses also stipulated that the mileage be given. Mileposts of cast iron followed and this one at Coldwall Bridge records Cheadle 11 miles and the date 1822 on an iron plate. Today this once important route into Staffordshire is grass-covered and quiet and here the author sat and speculated on how the word mile originated. It is explained in England's first road book, John Ogilby's *Britannia* which was compiled towards the end of the 17th century on the instructions of Charles II. It states – '*The Romans accounted by miles and stadia, the mile containing precisely 1,000 paces of five foot, and the stadia or furlong 125 paces. Thus the Roman mile of 1,000 (mille) paces of five foot gave the name to our mile, and it should be pointed out that the Roman pace was measured from the heel to heel of the same foot - i.e. two paces*'. It is curious that our word mile should come from the Roman *mille* but no less strange that our measure of inches began with the inch as the length of three barley-corns! An excuse is made for this digression into the fascinating origin of our land measures, for a number of milestones from the Roman through to the guidestones and cast iron types will be found in the county, and it was good to see in the 1997 Winter Number of *Greenwatch*, the environmental newspaper of the County Council, a call for Parish Councils and other groups to keep milestones in good condition.

149 Preserved Tollgates C2

When the Turnpike Trusts were set up at the beginning of the 18th century to keep the roads in good repair tolls were charged and tollhouses and gates built at specific points. Although almost all the gates have disappeared many tollhouses still remain (no. 81) and so do many gateposts, now put to other uses – they are round with a mushroom top. This example has been preserved by the Peak District National Park and stands beside the Bamford Road near the *Marquis of Granby*. A plaque nearby states that it was set up in 1985 and originally stood on the Sheffield to Manchester Road which was turnpiked in 1724. A new bar has been provided and it has three posts with a small gateway for pedestrians.

150 Fair Flora   D3

This graceful statue has stood in Stoke
Wood near Grindleford for over 150
years, arousing curiosity and becoming the
subject of various legends. One
explanation is that it came from
Chatsworth House and was given to the
owner of Stoke Hall nearby. But why
Flora, the Roman goddess of flowers,
should now stand in a clearing in this
lonely wood is a mystery.

151 Styles in Stiles   C2

The narrow V stile common in
Derbyshire sometimes has a circular
clearance cut at the bottom as clearance
for the boot while others have clearance
for the hips, but this example has a very
large opening for a bucket. The reason for
this is that it gives access to an enclosure
which houses the villagers' water supply.
It stands at Bamford in the northern
Derwent Valley and may be the only
example in the county. A similar
enclosure at Monyash also houses the
telephone kiosk, but here there is the
usual narrow V stile and buckets have to
be lifted onto the flat-topped walls when
passing through.

152 Village's own Water
Company   C5

This water reservoir standing in the centre
of Youlgreave Village is called Conduit
Head, but affectionately known in the
village as *The Fountain*. As can be seen it
was erected in 1829, prior to which, water
was carried from the River Bradford in
the dale far below. Today the village is
one of a very few which has its own water
company, independent of the Severn Trent
Water Company. The site of the conduit
was originally occupied by a Saxon cross,
and one wonders if its base is the one now
preserved in the churchyard.

153 Thimble Hall C5

This tiny cottage stands behind Conduit Head in Youlgreave shown in the previous photograph. With only one up and one down, Thimble Hall, as it is called, was inhabited until a few years ago since when it has been used as a store place. Each room is less than 8 feet square and there is a fixed ladder to the bedroom and a stone fireplace, also exposed beams and exposed floorboards in the bedroom. Today it is a source of amusement and curiosity and a Grade II listed building. In September 1999 it was sold at auction for an astounding £39,500!

154 Pulp Millstones D5

Travellers along Holestone Road which crosses the hills west of Ashover may be intrigued by the name of an isolated farm there. It is called Old Engine Farm and a visit revealed the name came from a lead mine there shown on the map as New Engine Mine! (a new engine had been installed). I am indebted to Mr Malcolm Wragg, owner of the farm for showing me the mine shaft which is 365 yards deep, and also a shallow drift mine nearby which meanders around but does not connect with the shaft. There is now no evidence of the engine which pumped water from the mine, but curiosity is aroused by a row of millstones which stand beside the farm drive. As can be seen they are very wide, unlike those used in the wind- and water-mills for they worked upright as in the case of the cider mill (no. 96). These were not used for crushing apples, however, but for pulping paper and were known as 'pulp' stones. The 'cores' or centres cut from the stones were not wasted and examples may be seen built into the walls of the farm. The 'trough' seen in the foreground of Old Engine Farm is from the rough block of stone from which a stone had been cut.

155 A Wall in Darley Dale D5

As seen in this photograph the 'cores' from pulp millstones shown in the previous photograph were not only used for building materials. This wall near Darley Bridge in Darley Dale has two rows of cores built into it which help to relieve the flood waters from the nearby River Derwent which frequently overflows its banks.

156 Birchover Porch D5

A more decorative use for the 'cores' from pulp millstones is seen in this photograph of a porch at Birchover. Besides the conventional type of millstones, pulp stones were made in the quarries on Stanton Moor above the village, and other villagers have used the cores from them in their gardens and thus preserved a little of the history of the mills.

157 Joseph Paxton's Station D4

Visitors to Peak Village, the Outlet Shopping Centre at Rowsley may wonder at the fine old building at its centre, which although built in 1849 does not look out of place among the modern buildings. These are made of a similar stone, and the old station, for such it was, looks well as a centrepiece. Today it is an Ice Cream Parlour and Confectionery and shown on the map there simply as *The Station*, and it would be of interest if some history of this prestigious building were given, for it was designed by Sir Joseph Paxton designer of the Crystal Palace. He was head gardener for the Duke of Devonshire and designed it for the Duke at the time when the Midland Railway intended to continue the line up the Derwent Valley and through Chatsworth Park. When the route was changed to go through Bakewell a new station was built at Rowsley and Paxton's station left high and dry. For a time it served as the terminus for a short branch line and the area put to various uses. The main line through Bakewell opened up the beauty of Monsal Dale, Millers Dale and Chee Dale, but this in turn was closed by Beeching in 1967-68. Now the Monsal Trail, it is hoped to re-open this line.

158 High Peak Railway C5

The Cromford and High Peak Railway, to give it its full title, connected the Cromford Canal in the Derwent Valley with the Peak Forest Canal near Buxworth north of Buxton (nos. 15-16). It was engineered by Josias Jessop and opened in 1830-31. It passed through the short Newhaven Tunnel beneath the Ashbourne to Buxton road, and here on the northern entrance a plaque has the contractor's initials, while a similar plaque on the southern entrance has the names of the engineer and clerk. Today this route is the very popular High Peak Trail and not far from the tunnel it is joined by the Tissington Trail, a lovely walk down to Ashbourne.

159 Clay Cross Coal F5

When George Stephenson built the North Midland Railway between Derby and Leeds he tunnelled beneath Clay Cross. Now a small town, this was at that time a hamlet, and being situated on the ridge between the Rivers Amber and Rother a tunnel was necessary. Although only just over one mile long the cutting of this proved fortuitous, for Stephenson struck a coal seam and iron ore and lost no time in exploiting this and founded George Stephenson and Company which later became Clay Cross Company. The shape of the tunnel is an upright oval in section, and curiously each entrance is of a different design, the southern seen here being unadorned while the northern is in the style of a Moorish gateway with castellated towers built to commemorate the Clay Cross Company's success. Unfortunately this is now embraced within a large industrial complex and difficult to find, but the southern entrance stands near the church at the southern approach to the town.

160 Tunnel Ventilators in Clay Cross   F5

With the discovery of coal and iron ore Clay Cross grew rapidly into an engineering and colliery town and a line of ventilating shafts along the route of the tunnel has now been embraced within its busy streets. These plain brick towers – this one has been painted white – no doubt puzzle people passing through the town, but residents know that they are evidence of an event which changed the town's fortunes.

161 Ornamental Brickwork C8

Bricklayers sometimes give way to their fancies with the use of different coloured bricks to commemorate events in dates or letters. An interesting variation is seen in this farm building at Longford Hall where the initials WC and the date are formed by missing bricks. Together with other designs fashioned in a similar way they give an attractive lacework effect and also give ventilation to the building. The Coke family lived at the hall nearby for nearly 300 years and there are many memorials to them in the church here. Notable was Thomas William Coke who became an MP and Father of the House and was known as the handsome Englishman. He was made 5th Earl of Leicester and became famous as an agriculturalist, and one wonders if he was the WC picked out on the end of the barn. However he was born in 1752 and died in 1842 and the date 1760 thus seems to have no significance – could he have laid the first brick when he was 8, I wonder?

162 Trademarks in Brick D11

Sometimes the function of a building is shown by a symbol formed by raised bricks and there are examples of the blacksmith having a doorway in the shape of a horseshoe. Derbyshire has none, but at Lullington in the far south of the county a building still has a horseshoe symbol in raised brickwork on its gable end. In the next building close by, a joiner's shop is indicated in a similar way by a square and compass, a fine example of the bricklayer's craft.

163 Heage Windmill E6

Although there are a number of ruined windmills still standing in the county there is only one complete with sails, the *Cat and Fiddle*, a post mill overlooking Dale Abbey east of Derby. Now, however, the fine tower of Heage Mill which has graced Dungeley Hill since the end of the 18th century is to be completely restored. It closed in 1916 and stood derelict as seen here for many years until it was bought in the 1960s by the Derbyshire County Council, who invested £36,000 in repairs and restoration. It is a Grade II Listed Building. Its sails were rebuilt, but without their shutters, and the cap and fantails restored, but unfortunately it suffered damage by lightning losing two of its sails. The County Council together with the Heage Windmill Society applied for a grant to the Heritage Lottery Fund resulting in a grant of £164, 000. The Windmill Society and local firms have contributed financially, the Society also providing voluntary labour. The whole restoration will cost £300,000 – £350,000 and it is hoped to restore the mill to working order with a small visitor centre early in the new millennium. It will once again be a striking landmark seen from far and wide.

Another derelict tower mill which has been restored, this time as a dwelling stands close by the Chesterfield to Matlock road above Kelstedge. It has no commanding position or sails or fantail and its cap has been replaced by a roof. Nevertheless it is a very pleasant sight, and it is good to see yet another reminder of a past way of life preserved.

164 South Normanton Windmill F5

Unlike the restored mills in the previous entries which are such prominent and attractive features, the ruined mill at South Normanton is almost hidden by the church tower. It has lost its cap and sails, and in its latter years was driven by steam and one wonders if its performance as a 'wind' mill was affected by its proximity to the church tower. One is reminded of the two tower mills called James and Sarah which stood close together at Riddings until a few years ago; they were so close James stole all the wind and Sarah never did work! This mill at South Normanton is not like the usual sturdier types with tapered sides but has almost vertical walls and perhaps this was the reason for the strengthening iron bands, for there would be strong vibrations when the sails were turning. Like dovecotes and icehouses and other reminders of a past way of life, windmills have a fascinating history. Originally owned by the Lord of the Manor and run by the miller, they were later owned privately by the miller. He acquired a bad reputation, often accused of giving short weight of flour for the grain taken to him and also of adding extraneous matter to the flour. It was said that hair grows on the palm of the honest miller, and it was asked '*What is the bravest thing in the world?*' the answer being '*a miller's shirt for it holds a thief by the throat every day*'. That there was some justification for his reputation is found in documents recording that some millers were restricted in the number of fowls and pigs they were allowed to keep!

165 St. Brides Tympanum   E9

The intriguing name St. Brides is shown on the Landranger Ordnance Map about one mile west of Melbourne. St. Brides is a farm standing on the site of a chapel of Burton Abbey, and old records show that several footpaths converged here. This wealthy abbey once held land around south Derbyshire as well as in over nine other counties. Old maps also record that

stone coffins have been unearthed but the only evidence seen today is a tiny Norman tympanum built into the front of the farmhouse. As seen here it is badly worn, but the shape of an animal can be discerned. I am indebted to the owner of the farm for his kind permission to take the photograph and also that of the double cheese press shown in photograph no. 103.

166 Ticknall's Old Water Supply   E9

The tympanum at St. Brides shown above is not esay to find, but these attractive standpipes which dot the roadside in Ticknall village not far away cannot be missed. These taps were erected by Sir Harpur Crewe of Calke Abbey in 1914, Ticknall being an 'estate' village although today many of the houses are owned by the former tenants. In the 1950s piped water was introduced but some of the taps are still in use. Made of cast iron they are complete with a stand and a handle seen on the top right, the water issuing from the mouth of a lion's head. The lockup (no.2) is not far away but easily missed, close by a lane which branches up to the church seen on the next page.

167 Ticknall's Old Church E9

Ticknall village lies astride the A514 about two miles west of St. Brides. On entering the churchyard, curiosity is aroused by a large block of masonry there, all that remains of the former church of St. Thomas of Canterbury. This was demolished in 1840 to make way for the new church of St. James erected two years later and mainly financed by Sir George Crewe; yet another designed by Derby's H.I.Stevens (no. 77). The old church built in the 14th century, was in poor repair and too small for the rising population when the village was a hive of activity with lime kilns and pot works. It was well built and gunpowder was used, not entirely successfully, and now this portion which remains is listed as an Ancient Monument. It is good to see this evidence of the old church retained, also the taps in the village shown on the previous page. The village cross seen in the foreground here was moved into the churchyard when the attractive almshouses near the gates were built. A tablet records they were built by Charles Harpur in 1772 to house seven 'Decayed House-keepers'!

168 Melbourne Pool   F9

Ticknall Brook feeds Melbourne Pool about three miles downstream from Ticknall and one shouldn't visit south Derbyshire without seeing historic Melbourne village. The fine hall has extensive gardens – you must go on an 'open' day to see curiosity no. 106 - and close by is St. Michael and St. Mary church described by Pevsner as 'one of the most ambitious Norman parish churches in England'. Beyond is the Pool where once stood a corn mill from which Melbourne took its name (mill-bourne) and a later mill which still stands is now a residence. When Queen Victoria gave her name to the Australian state she named its capital after her Prime Minister, Lord Melbourne who had taken his title from this Derbyshire village. Strange that a great city twelve thousand miles away should be named after a corn mill in a little English village. In the 14th century Melbourne had a castle and legend has it

that the stone for it came from a quarry which now lies beneath the pool. Castle Street and Castle Square are nearby, but one looks in vain for signs of a castle for they are slight and lie behind Castle Mills. It was still inhabited in the 16th century, but then, as with so many similar buildings, it was used as a quarry. The county has little such evidence of its Norman castles, as at Horsley and Duffield, but has a fine pseudo example as seen on the next page.

Foundations of Melbourne Castle

94

169 Bolsover Castle F4

This striking castle, standing high on the hills east of Chesterfield, presents a picture-book scene to travellers on the M1 Motorway, in the valley far below. The Keep, seen here, built in the Norman style on the site of a previous Norman Keep, could easily be mistaken for a castle of that period. Bess of Hardwick of Hardwick Hall and Chatsworth House fame began the building and it was completed by her son Sir Charles Cavendish in 1613. His son Sir William – Baron Cavendish of Bolsover and Duke of Newcastle were among his many titles – continued building and the family's wealth and standing are shown when he entertained Charles I in 1633, the dinner alone costing £4,000. When the Queen visited the castle later the cost was over £14,000. Such was the splendour of Bolsover which is now in ruins and open to the public, its Keep having been restored.

170 An Indoor Riding School F4

Among the extensive building by Sir William Cavendish at Bolsover Castle is the Riding School seen here. He had a reputation for classical riding and had written several books on the subject, and when he entertained Charles I and his Queen one may assume that they rode here together.

Society which, founded in 1894, was one of the oldest in Britain. In 1932 a mass trespass from the *Snake Inn* resulted in five ramblers being arrested and gaoled, an event which contributed to the opening of a large area of Kinder Scout through access agreements with several landowners, and in 1997 the society held a special celebratory walk over the route. Parts of the moors are preserved for grouse and closed at certain times of the year and respect should be shown to all these restrictions. Each year 22 million people visit the Peak District and many will walk the 1,600 miles of footpaths there, and when the author walked this path from the *Snake Inn* to Hayfield recently he found it well worn but it should not be taken lightly, especially in bad weather. The wild scenery has not changed and together with the lovely limestone dales and the pastoral scenes of the Trent Valley it emphasises the great variety in the county.

171 An Historic Signpost
A2

In this last curiosity we leap across the county from Bolsover near the eastern border to Hayfield near where the book started at New Mills on the western side. In between are many of the features shown here, and as some of these can only be found on foot the author is happy to include this evidence of the work of the early pioneers in walking in Derbyshire. This signpost is one of several similar in the Peak District, and stands beside the secondary road in Hayfield which ends at the Kinder Reservoir. It arouses interest and curiosity for it commemorates an important event on May 29th 1897 when a party of ramblers met at the *Snake Inn* on the Snake Pass and walked over Kinder Scout to emerge here in Hayfield, a distance of six miles through some of the wildest and loneliest countryside in England. It was organised by the Peak District and Northern Counties Footpaths

Walkers approach William Clough near Hayfield.